MW00579334

A ROAD TO BOUNTIFUL

Chris —

I hope you enjoy the stories in the book, but also take a look at the bonus material on page 143.

Please let me know if I can ever provide you with some free advice and opinion regarding your real estate efforts!

Harry

(614) 774-0300

ALSO BY GARRETT K. SCANLON

Walking and Talking: Stories of Success and Humor in the Real Estate World of Business

Lead Like Reagan: Principles of Dynamic Leadership

Seeing Past Friday Night

Single Page Life Plan

Single Page Life Plan for Realtors

A ROAD TO BOUNTIFUL

28 Paths from China That Led to a Fruitful Partnership in Real Estate

GARRETT K. SCANLON

BALLYLONGFORD BOOKS

Ballylongford Books
2588 Welsford Road
Columbus, Ohio 43221

Scanlon, Garrett K.

A road to bountiful : 28 paths from China that led to a fruitful partnership in real estate / Garrett K. Scanlon. — Columbus, Ohio : Ballylongford Books, [2015]

pages ; cm.

ISBN: 978-0-9961943-5-8

1. Chinese—United States—Anecdotes. 2. Real estate investment—United States. 3. Chinese Americans—Economic conditions. 4. Success in business—United States. 5. Entrepreneurship—United States. 6. Chinese—United States—Economic conditions. 7. Real estate investment—United States—Finance. 8. Immigrants—United States— Economic conditions. 9. Real estate investment—Syndication—United States. 10. Real estate investment trusts—United States. I. Title

E184.C5 S33 2015 2015946171
305.8951/073—dc23 1509

PRINTED AND BOUND IN THE UNITED STATES OF AMERICA
FIRST PRINTING 2015

Garrett K. Scanlon is available for training, consulting, and speaking. Visit www.GarrettScanlon.com to bring him to your company, group, school, or nonprofit organization.

Front cover design by www.kristinecoplin.com
Jacket and text design by www.tothepointsolutions.com

Disclaimer

The stories, facts, anecdotes, examples, suggestions, and opinions stated in this book by the author are subject to errors and omissions. Readers should rely solely on the reader's expertise, and the expertise of reader's legal, accounting, and financial counsel regarding the purchase, sale, management and/or ownership of real estate. Author assumes no responsibility for the investments made by the reader, and shall not be responsible or held liable to any person or entity with respect to any loss or damage caused, or alleged to have been caused, directly or indirectly, by the information contained herein. Author does not represent the reader in the purchase, sale, management, or exchange of investment real estate. Always consult with your attorney and your accountant when involving yourself in real estate.

Any mention of companies or individuals in this book is not an endorsement of same, and author is not responsible for any real estate investments made by the reader, now or in the future.

Although the publisher and the author have made an effort to safeguard that information in this book was correct at the time of publication, the author and publisher of this book do not assume and hereby disclaim any liability to any party for any loss, damage, or disruption caused by errors, or omissions, or opinions, whether such errors or omissions, or opinions result from negligence, accident, or any other cause. Market conditions of all kinds regarding supply, demand, changes of interest rates, rental rates, returns on investment, pricing, cash flow, tax consequence, management policies, etc. are beyond the control of the author, and the author makes no predictions regarding how any or all of these will present themselves in the future. Every reader and every investor is different, and the advice and strategies contained herein may not be suitable for your situation.

Dedicated to all of the *bountiful partners* who are profiled in this book. You dream heroic dreams. Your faith, hope, and optimism helps to build a better future for us all.

Contents

BONUS MATERIAL: FUNDAMENTALS OF MULTIFAMILY INVESTMENT REAL ESTATE

Preface

I have spent over thirty years in the real estate industry and have had the good fortune of working with some of the most interesting and talented people from all walks of life.

These are people from the diverse industries of real estate, medicine, insurance, law, hospitality, law enforcement, advertising, and civic enterprise. I am always fascinated and encouraged by their leadership qualities and their entrepreneurial spirit.

Their hard work, determination, and creativity motivate me to write about the sacrifices they make and the successes they achieve. I consider them to be *heroes of the marketplace.* They venture into the world of real estate, accept the risk and uncertainty that comes with it, and assemble a team of talented experts to help them achieve their goals.

This book highlights a group of such people, who for one reason or another, gravitated towards each other to form a partnership to purchase investment real estate. The title of this book, *A Road to Bountiful*, was chosen because, from many different paths, they all converged upon a road that has led them to a place of fruitful friendship and financial reward. Along the way, it has allowed them to give back to their community and to pave an abundant pathway upon which the next generation may travel.

Throughout their journey, there have been challenges, detours, and learning curves. On the following pages, you will read their stories. This book begins with *Partner Profiles* and is followed by other real estate stories and conversations that will give you an interesting glimpse into the fascinating world of real estate.

I hope you enjoy!

Acknowledgments

I would like to thank all of the *bountiful partners* who are profiled in this book. This book could not have been written without your patient and friendly help.

Thank you Mary Jo Zazueta, of To The Point Solutions, for designing the interior of the book and cover work. You are always incredibly professional and it is always a great pleasure to work with you.

Thank you Bethany Jones for helping me with various edits of the text that improved this book.

Thank you Kristine Coplin for your graphic design work. You are tremendously creative with an eye for detail.

I would also like to thank Milli DeVenne, Mikey DeVenne, and Lita Scanlon for giving me good ideas and inspiration to write this book.

Thank you Terry Kelley for reading through yet another manuscript. You always make needed corrections and add important insight. Thanks Cousin Terrence!

A special thank you to Jeva Lin and Bobby Yu for helping me bring *A Road to Bountiful* to fruition. It is always a pleasure and an honor to be with you and all of your *bountiful partners*, as you travel your journey together.

A ROAD TO BOUNTIFUL

Partner Profile

Jeva Lin

Planting the Seed

Few things surprise me in the world of real estate, but I was shocked the day Jeva Lin called me to say that the apartments she and her husband, Bobby, had recently purchased, were 100% occupied with tenants.

Only six weeks earlier, in the middle of a harsh winter season, they had closed on the purchase of a 16-unit apartment building that had eight vacancies. There were several other owners in the same area who were competing against them to attract new renters on those cold and snowy days.

Cold weather certainly plays a role in attracting new tenants and Jeva and Bobby had planted their first seed of investment when it was difficult to attract new renters.

I said to Jeva at the closing, "Jeva, when the weather thaws, you will begin to see increased customer traffic from potential renters. You should probably plan on filling your building by the end of June."

Jeva replied, "Oh, I don't think it will take that long, Garry." I attributed her over-confidence to a lack of experience. When she called and announced that she had filled the entire building in six weeks, I was astounded! But then again, I didn't know Jeva's history.

Cultural Shock

President Reagan was finishing up his last term in the White House and the economy was strong when Jeva Lin arrived in New York City in the late 80s. She remembers her first full day in America very clearly.

"I followed my Aunt through Chinatown, as she knocked on doors looking for a place for me to work. By late morning, I was hired to bus tables at a Chinese restaurant in a Manhattan hotel. My Aunt told me, 'Good… now we have to find you a place to rent!' So, that afternoon she found me a place to live. We shopped for groceries, and I moved in that very night! It all happened so fast."

Jeva was pre-enrolled in school and had a full schedule right from the beginning. Each day she would walk to the restaurant at 5:30 am and work the breakfast shift until 10 o'clock. From there she would walk to Hunter College where she attended classes from 11:00 in the morning until 4:00 in the afternoon.

Had it been me, I probably would have walked home from there, had dinner, done some homework, and congratulated myself on having put in such a strong day! But for Jeva, the end of classes each day only signaled that it was time to walk the 5 long blocks to Upper Manhattan, where she would bus tables at another restaurant until closing time. Arriving home at midnight, she would prepare to do the same thing all over again the next day.

"Eventually," says Jeva, "I found a better job, on 34th Street, working as a cashier at a restaurant that specialized in delivering Chinese meals to local businesses."

Three years later, as she was finishing up her college studies, Jeva was approached by a group of restaurateurs who asked her to help them open up new locations.

"My job was to find good locations, negotiate the leases, and hire contractors to remodel the existing space into a nice restaurant. I would then train the staff to operate the day-to-day activity. After we established a reputation for great food and good service, we would oftentimes sell the business."

All of this was typically done within the span of a single year. Jeva participated in the equity of these ventures and successfully opened several restaurants in Brooklyn, Upper State New York, and various cities in Ohio.

In 1994, Jeva focused her energies on earning an MBA in Finance. To accomplish this goal as quickly as possible, she attended two different schools at the same time (The University of Saint Francis in Indiana during the day, and The University of Findlay at night). She earned her degree in a single year.

Then she returned to China.

A Second Cultural Shock

According to Jeva, "It was a huge cultural shock for me when I came from China to the United States. When I returned to China, for me, it was a *second* cultural shock! So many things had changed so quickly, and China had grown so much, I didn't seem to fit in the same way I had remembered. It was like a reverse cultural shock."

Jeva taught large groups of people about the art of entrepreneurial techniques. While she enjoyed what she was doing, she decided to return to the United States in 1997.

"Initially, I took a job in Mansfield, Ohio selling shoes and clothing. But, one day, a lady who was shopping at the store was impressed by my customer service skills and she recommended me to a local bank. They hired me as a bank teller."

And then things started happening on Jeva's birthdays.

"On my birthday that same year, Bobby read in the paper that a local boat manufacturing company was looking to hire an entry level accountant. He said, 'Jeva, that's the same company

Judy works for!' Judy was our next-door neighbor and a very dear friend of ours. The next day, we asked her if she could find out from her HR department if they were still hiring. At midnight, that very day, we heard someone knocking at our front door. It was Judy! She said, 'You have to give me a resume right away!' And that is how I got the job!

Within a couple of years, Jeva rose to become CFO of the company, obtained her Oracle license, and was certified as a Data Base Administrator. She was placed in charge of the IT and Accounting Departments. It was an exciting time for Jeva, as she was able to implement innovative systems due to the advent of new computer technology.

"Working with the various department leaders, I was able to build an intranet system throughout the entire plant that allowed people to share blueprints, receive work flow instructions, and develop management policies via our computer system," recalls Jeva.

The Move to Columbus

As Jeva and Bobby's success grew, so did their family! They now had three daughters, the oldest of whom was approaching high school age. Jeva became concerned that their children could be at risk of losing their identity with their Chinese ancestry that Jeva and Bobby value so much.

"I have always been aware that Columbus has a strong Chinese community, and the idea of moving there to maintain that cultural connection was very appealing to us," says Jeva. "However, Bobby had been employed with the same company for 20 years and he wanted *both* of us to acquire jobs in Columbus before making a move. Bobby enjoyed living in Mansfield and was reluctant to leave."

But Jeva was anxious to move *quickly*. She says, "Gina was approaching her freshman year in high school, so I knew that if we didn't move right then, we would likely end up waiting another 4 years, until she graduated."

So, in typical Jeva fashion, she *created* a couple of jobs for her and Bobby... as real estate investors! On a cold winter day in 2004, she and Bobby met my father, Jim Scanlon, who presented them with their first multifamily investment property; that 16 unit, garden-style apartment building that was half vacant and priced accordingly.

Jeva recalls, "We needed to plant financial stakes in Columbus before Bobby would move. Investing in Columbus property did that for us."

And then came another birthday!

This time it was 2005 and Jeva celebrated that day by accepting a position with AEP as a Financial and IT Auditor in a department that trades commodities. It was then that they decided to *literally* plant stakes in Columbus.

"We found a plot of ground on which to build a house. There were many issues involved with the construction of the home and I wanted to learn more about every facet of real estate. So, I went to school at Hondros College to learn more. This led me to obtaining my real estate license, and the formation of Spring Property Management, my real estate brokerage." says Jeva.

Soon, Jeva began to perform property management for other apartment owners who had witnessed how well she managed her own properties. Referrals began to pour in.

When Jeva and Bobby saw an opportunity to purchase a 96 unit apartment community, they decided to take the leap and add the property to their portfolio. This provided them with the economies of scale to grow their business quickly.

And then came another birthday for Jeva.

Creating Economies of Scale

On *that* birthday, she decided to go *full-time* into real estate. It seemed a natural progression at that point to begin forming partnerships with their friends and acquaintances. Today, Jeva and Bobby manage over 1,000 apartments in Central Ohio and

New York City; a combination of apartments that they own, manage for others, or have purchased with fellow investors.

As their business continues to grow, Jeva and Bobby ensure that it only grow at a pace that is consistent with the availability of great property.

"We never want to buy real estate just for the sake of doing another transaction. We choose every property based upon its location, the anticipated growth in that area, and how it fits in with our style of property management. We also put a great emphasis on getting the most favorable financing terms that are available. We consider ourselves to be patient investors, waiting for the right opportunities," Jeva says.

"What I like about real estate," she says, "is that it enables us to work around the kid's schedule. And you meet a lot of different people from all walks of life; lenders, attorneys, brokers, the tenants you lease to, the managers you hire...everyone!"

Combining Unique Strengths

And Jeva is grateful that she has Bobby as a great partner.

"You know me, Garry. I am very intense. I stay focused on the documents, the numbers, and all of the detail work. I have a very exact nature, which sometimes translates to others as demanding. Bobby is much more laid back than I am. He is a great people person. We balance each other out."

According to Jeva, there is very little communication required between the two of them.

"There is an unspoken understanding between us. Bobby actively searches for good properties that we should acquire. I am the calculator. I confirm if the numbers will work. Bobby oversees all of the maintenance issues and brings his unique people skills into the equation. I put the systems in place for the work procedures, monthly reports, banking activity ... things like that. Both of us share the responsibility of maximizing the return for the investors."

Setting an Example for the Next Generation

Jeva believes that their daughters have benefited from the entrepreneurial direction she and Bobby have taken.

"I think they see how hard we work and have a respect for the effort it takes to be successful. And, we have also been able to provide them with a great education."

Jeva also lets her kids get some hands-on experience in the field.

"Gina, for instance, prepares rent rolls and other types of computer input. She also gets a chance to hear me in my discussions with other people and see how I conduct various meetings. It helps her to learn how to read other people, and it gives her an idea on how everything fits together. She is taking real estate classes now so that she will be able to sit for her exam and get her real estate license when she turns 21."

Maybe on her birthday!

Jeva and Bobby have also enjoyed providing internships for some of the children of friends they have met at their church or at the Chinese school. With a strong faith in God, and a respect for her Chinese heritage, Jeva relishes the times she spends with others in the Chinese community. A dream of hers is to one day help establish a multi-purpose facility in Central Ohio, where Chinese families can gather for schooling, dining, shopping, medical assistance, and day care needs. It would certainly be a long way from her humble beginnings in New York City.

A Walk-in Closet

Recently, I was with Jeva as she gave an appraiser a tour of one of the model apartments that she manages. She stopped in front of a large walk-in closet and smiled at us.

"That is almost the exact size of my first apartment in Manhattan, Garry!"

While a lot of things have changed since her first day in New York, Jeva's adherence to the principles of hard work and education, and her willingness to seize opportunities, continues to serve her well. That is why I was not surprised when I Jeva began purchasing additional apartments; this time in Manhattan!

This started when one of the multi-story townhouses that Jeva used to walk by during her early days in New York became available. When she and her partners closed on that property, I could only think to myself, *there she goes again, planting another seed*!

Partner Profile

Bobby Yu

A Third Income

I have always been fascinated by personality studies that are based upon a person's birth order within the family. There are, of course the *first-borns*; those high achievers who have a reputation for being very well organized and having strong leadership skills. Then, there are the youngest children; those who are accustomed to being pampered a bit and showered with attention. They tend to be the creative risk takers who have a good sense of humor and like to entertain.

And, of course, we have the middle children. Bobby Yu (Jeva's husband) and I both fall into this category. Both of us grew up with two older siblings and two younger siblings. Most social experts would say that we have an inclination towards artistic expression; that we tend to be easy going and even tempered. In Bobby's case, that certainly seems to be true. But, more about that later.

Archie Griffin was picking up first downs for the Bengals and Tom Seaver was hurling 90 mile-per-hour fastballs for the Reds in the early 80s, when a 16-year-old boy named Bobby Yu, arrived in Cincinnati, Ohio. His grandfather, who had been a resident of that city for more than 5 decades, served as a mentor to Bobby.

As a young person, Bobby always dreamed of opening a restaurant. This is how he eventually ended up meeting his future wife, Jeva Lin.

"Jeva and I were both running restaurants at the time," Bobby recalls. "In the 90s there was an explosion of new restaurants, popping up all around the city. So, we decided to sell our restaurants at about the same time and get married."

Three Kids? Three Incomes!

Soon, they were raising their 3 young children, Gina, Rae, and Ona. It was then that Bobby decided that they needed to begin thinking about generating a third income.

According to Bobby, "A lot of people who don't think about a third income are very vulnerable. They are often surprised when one of them ends up having to change jobs due to a layoff, a relocation, or the closing of a business. They end up burning through a lot of their saving before they land that next job. If you don't have any kids, this isn't a big concern. But, once those kids come along, you need to start looking for that third income!"

It was this quest for a third income that motivated Jeva and Bobby to invest in real estate. Their first purchase of an apartment provided lessons in ownership that Bobby will use for a lifetime.

"We had two residents who didn't want to pay rent. But, they didn't want to *leave* either," says Bobby. "That's even *worse* than having vacancies! And we had several of those too."

Through a series of trials and errors, Bobby taught himself how to operate the apartments.

'Hands-On' Learning

Bobby says, "Maintenance isn't very difficult. If you just keep trying, you eventually figure it out. You build up experience as you go. There is really no better way to learn, other than to just get in there and do it."

Bobby believes that it is vital for real estate investors to always stay persistent.

"The single biggest mistake people sometimes make is that they don't see the light at the end of the tunnel. They get almost all the way to a successful venture, and then give up. They get so close, but don't realize how close they are to achieving the goal. No matter what, you have to stick with it. No matter how hard it is along the way, if you see it through, you will succeed, guaranteed!"

Bobby laughs about the time he was reminded of just how difficult those early days were.

Bobby recalls, "About 4 years after getting into real estate, I inspected one of the units that a resident had recently vacated. I called Jeva on the phone, very upset.

I said, 'Jeva, you will not believe what I just saw. Whoever painted this apartment last time did a terrible job. They even painted over the baseboards! Find out who did this and call me back.' A few minutes later, Jeva called me on my cell phone, and said, 'I found out who painted that unit. It was you!' I was shocked. But then I thought about it, and realized that it was the first apartment I ever painted, in that original building."

A Belief in Plans, Policies, and Systems

Bobby is a big believer in having a comprehensive maintenance plan.

He says, "There are two things you have to do. First, always respond quickly to any issue the resident has. Then, do it right the first time. Don't rush through it. Don't take any shortcuts. If you think things through, and do things correctly, this will always save you money in the long run."

Bobby is also a strong advocate for adhering to policies that are set in place.

A Big Mistake

"I have learned to trust the systems that Jeva has created. Years ago, I made a big mistake. Despite Jeva's insistence that we always check the credit of a potential renter, I made an exception. One night, I signed a lease with someone who offered to prepay for the first three months. It was after hours, and I thought to myself, *how bad could this person's credit be if he's willing to pay rent upfront*?"

Bobby discovered that a person who deals drugs will offer to prepay rent to prevent any past criminal activity from being revealed by a background check.

"Fortunately," says Bobby, "the guy agreed to leave, and we didn't have any trouble. But, from that point on, I have always stayed within the parameters of Jeva's policies."

Bobby says that some of the best advice he could offer others is to have partners who complement each other.

Which gets us back to the personality characteristics of Bobby Yu, a middle child.

The Yin and Yang Theory

"I tend to be more laid back and less organized. Jeva, on the other hand, is more straightforward, and structured. I am more of a mediator; more encouraging. Jeva is more abrupt, more exact in her approach. All of these qualities have their place. So, if you have partners who fill in for each other's strengths and weaknesses, things work out very well."

As an example, Bobby says, "For instance, if you have two partners who both love to golf, they will get along very well. But, who is taking care of things when they are both out playing golf at the same time? One of the partners has to say, 'Forget the golf today. There are things that need to be tended to right now.'"

For Bobby, good communication seems to be the key. "Don't be afraid to ask a lot of questions. You're relying on each other's expertise."

***Owning* the Job!**

What he likes best about real estate is that it is a physical, tangible asset that throws off income.

According to Bobby, "It is hard to make a dollar; to work a job. With real estate, in a sense, you *own* the job. For me, I look at any difficulties that come with owning real estate as helpful reminders of the opportunities that exist when you have your own business. It's important to keep the right attitude, the right perspective."

I asked Bobby what is better: owning real estate by yourself, or owning real estate in partnership with other people.

"To me, it doesn't matter either way," he says. "I follow the same policies and procedures, regardless. I do it all the same way, and so does Jeva. You are limited in size, though, if you don't expand into partnerships. Both parties benefit from expanding the scope of the business. It helps you attract top personnel and gives you better buying power when you are negotiating with your vendors. As long as we maintain a good reputation for being honest and trustworthy, we will be successful," he says.

And, they will always have that third income.

Partner Profile

Frank and Anne M. Petit Wong

A Left-Behind Milk Bottle

It was during a table tennis tournament, that Frank Wong noticed a young lady named Anne, who was looking to procure a tennis racquet for her match. Frank did not know it at the time, but not only was Anne an outstanding table tennis player; she was also to become his wife.

When they were married in 1993, Frank was working as a cardiologist scholar at Boone Hospital Center. Anne, having earned her PhD in Plant Pathology from the University of Missouri, was attending Cornell University for her post-doctoral work.

Their participation in the fields of science and medicine was very natural for them, as both of them were from families with strong medical backgrounds.

Frank and Anne enjoyed their time in Columbia, Missouri. Frank continued to practice cardiology and Anne began her career in scientific research. During this time they were blessed with a new arrival, their daughter, Autumn. I asked how they had decided on such a pretty name.

"We had not yet picked out a name," recalls Anne, "but, when she was born on a very beautiful day in the fall, we decided to name her Autumn, which is *Pleasant Autumn* in Chinese."

Choosing a Midwestern City

When Anne changed her specialty from plant research to animal research, she received several outstanding job offers, one of which landed them in Chicago. Within a couple of years, management positions opened up in New York, Maine, and Ohio.

Frank and Autumn both liked the idea of living in a medium-sized Midwestern city, where the streets are a little wider and there is more green space devoted to yards, gardens, and parks. Anne knew she could be happy anywhere, as long as she enjoyed her job. So, on Autumn's 6th birthday, the Wong family arrived in Columbus, Ohio.

As Anne began her work at The Ohio State University, Frank became an early pioneer of entrepreneurs who studied and learned new technology in the United States that could be applied back in China, where he returned to start businesses to serve that market.

One early venture for Frank involved creating air purification systems that could be sold throughout China and Europe. This technology removed smoke and other pollutants from indoor air and became very popular in public places. Frank formed a partnership with two other people, and using letters from each of the partner's names, called it Walfen.

"We provided the research and development, obtained the needed patents and licenses, and created a procedure for meeting the manufacturing specifications required by the SFDA. We then leased this procedure to the actual manufacturing companies."

Eventually, it was Frank's natural skill at mechanical things that gave Anne the confidence to believe that they could operate investment real estate. But, in the beginning, it all started with a milk bottle and a cooler.

The Year-End Picnic

Anne is a volunteer teacher at a local Chinese Sunday School in Columbus, where she helps set the learning curriculum and organizes the training for teachers. It is here that she met Jeva Lin and Bobby Yu, and their family.

"All I really knew about Jeva," says Anne, "is that she held a managerial position at a boat manufacturing company, and that she and Bobby were obviously very dedicated to the Chinese school, as they had to travel 90 minutes each way for their children to attend."

"One day, the school was having its year-end picnic in the park. We were sitting together, and somehow, one of their milk bottles was mistakenly left in our cooler. I called Jeva on the phone and during that conversation we decided to get together at their home. Frank and Bobby discovered that they shared a common interest in building things, and the four of us soon became good friends."

"Jeva would sometimes talk about real estate that she owned, and once even suggested that Frank and I consider buying property ourselves. But, it would be another 2 years before I would begin asking more questions about it. The more I learned from Jeva, the more intrigued I became."

Entering the World of Business

Anne, whose father was a physician, continued. "You have to understand, Garry, that for my entire life, I never identified myself in any way as a business person. For me, it had always been about being a student, scholar, and researcher; being in the world of scientific academia. Frank was the one who knew and understood business. When Jeva told me that I too could succeed in business, it was hard for me to imagine. The idea of buying investment real estate was actually frightening in a way. It was unknown territory. And, some of the advice I got from others back then was very discouraging."

"Looking back, I think that many potential investors have a difficult time jumping into a business venture like real estate because they over-calculate. They look at the deal from so many different angles, that eventually, they find one that dissuades them. They are looking for an exactitude, which never really exists. Some people will say to me, 'What happens if the cash flow is not 8% as projected, but only 3%?' To which I respond, 'So what? 3% is better than zero!' In the end, Frank and I decided to buy because we trusted Jeva."

Frank concurs. "Yes, trust is everything, and we trusted Jeva and Bobby. I had just returned from a long trip from China, when Anne told me that she had picked out a building of 16 apartments for us to buy. It required us to liquidate some stock for the downpayment and we were going to be left with a large loan to pay back. I kept asking Anne, 'Why didn't you ask me about this? Why didn't you find out about that? Why are you so intent on doing this?'"

"Finally, she just looked at me and said, 'I just trust Jeva. I think this will work.' So, I agreed," says Frank.

From Stocks and Bonds to Sticks and Bricks

The timing for Frank and Anne's investment could not have been better. They sold their stock just before stock prices suddenly fell in 2007, and used that to buy the real estate.

Anne gave me a wonderful compliment when I asked her if she had received any valuable advice from others to help in her decision to invest in the property. She said, "Well, Jeva had given me the book you wrote, and I also read *Rich Dad Poor Dad*, which pointed out that, while I might be very well-educated, I was in many ways financially illiterate."

"But, Jeva taught me everything; how to lease, how to advertise, and how to finance the property. She taught me about tenant relations and how to keep the books and do the accounting. And, Frank is handy with everything. He learned very quickly from Bobby how to physically maintain the property. All of this gave me the confidence to go forward."

Frank laughs, "Sometimes when I am in China, Anne will call me for instructions on how to fix or replace a garbage disposal, and she will do it herself!"

Frank likes that he can focus on his hospital business in China, and can also enjoy the operational activities of the real estate in the states. "I like keeping busy," Frank says.

Since their original purchase, Frank and Anne have purchased additional real estate both individually, and in partnership with Jeva, Bobby, and their group of investors. They enjoy the camaraderie that comes with owning a property together.

Anne feels tremendously rewarded to have had the opportunity to take on a completely new challenge in her life, in the entirely different field of business.

"I have learned that business is not merely about money. Yes, it is important to be profitable. But, to achieve your business goals, money should be considered more of an offshoot of that success, rather than the sole goal."

"I am so grateful to have always been surrounded by good friends," says Anne. "Every single success I have had in my life can be linked to good friends and good mentors."

And maybe a left-behind milk bottle!

Partner Profile

Henry and Barbara Yan

Hobbies and Interests

Did I say something wrong?

That is what I was thinking when I saw Henry Yan's reaction to a question I had asked. He was explaining how, after earning an engineering degree from the University of Illinois, he had continued onto DePaul University for a degree in telecommunications. That's when I asked him:

"Henry, what kind of hobbies and interests did you pursue in your free time back then?"

Henry stared at me quizzically, probably wondering how I could have asked such a ridiculous question.

"Garry, I was working full time during the day at AT&T, going to school at night, and grading papers as a T.A. (Teacher's Assistant) on the weekends just to make ends meet. There *was* no free time."

After graduating from high school in the early 80s, Henry arrived as an international student with F-1 visa, and endured the financial burden of being on his own. After securing a job in a restaurant and finding an apartment in Chinatown, he began an 8-year journey of pursuing an education that would pay the bills and lead to a good job.

Career '*Choices*'

"Why did you decide on a career in science?" I asked.

"It was more a matter of *science* choosing *me*," he said. "In middle school, it was customary for students to be classified as being in the field of science or in liberal arts."

With a pharmacologist for a father, and a nurse for a mother, it was not surprising that Henry would wind up in the field of science. When reflecting on that time in his life, Henry recalls that it was all about working hard, studying, and striving to do his best; to get good grades, and maximize his potential.

Says Henry, "Our choice of work was based upon whatever we needed to do to survive economically. Finding a job that we really enjoyed was always secondary in importance."

From the *Windy City* to *C-Bus*!

When Henry's job in telecommunications brought him and his wife, Barbara, to Columbus, Ohio, it was somewhat of a culture shock.

"For nine years we had lived in Chicago where there are so many different things to do. We enjoyed, for instance, the multi-ethnic neighborhoods—Greektown, and Indiatown, and Chinatown. We liked the Chicago nightlife, with all of the entertainment and variety of restaurants. When we first moved to Columbus, it was so quiet that we would actually return to Chicago for the weekends!" says Henry.

"Soon, we began exploring other cities like Cincinnati, Cleveland, and Pittsburgh. Eventually we expanded our travels to New Orleans, Texas, all along the East Coast, and to Canada. Looking back, if we hadn't moved from Chicago, we probably wouldn't have gone to as many places as we did."

Henry smiled and said, "Of course, when our daughter Xuping Yan was born, all that changed. As you know, your children's activities become yours. So that brought the focus back to the local scene here in Columbus."

One of those activities included enrolling their daughter in one of the local Chinese schools on the weekends, where Henry and Barbara met and became good friends with Jeva Lin and Bobby Yu. When Barbara volunteered to help Jeva run the books during a period of time when Jeva was looking for some assistance, it helped her gain insight on some of the inner workings of the operation of Jeva's company. This, and Henry's desire to invest in real estate, resulted in a partnership with Jeva and Bobby to purchase apartments.

The Intrinsic Value of Real Estate

Henry says, "Real estate has always been appealing to me because of the intrinsic nature of its value. Even if the cash flow happens to decrease, the sticks and bricks and physical structure of your property cannot vanish overnight. You don't have that kind of assurance when you buy stock. You can make a lot of money in the stock market, but you can also lose a lot."

"My wife and I are very conservative, and we understand there is always risk. So, the first time Jeva and Bobby asked us to invest with them on a project, we decided not to. That first leap is tough. But, we regret that we didn't do that first deal. The next time they offered we said yes. We understood that there is risk with any investment, but we also knew they were good friends and knew for certain that everything would be handled in an honest manner."

Henry is happy to report, "Since then, we have used equity that was created from that first deal, and have applied it to other real estate we have purchased with Jeva and Bobby. As time has passed, we have become more and more comfortable with the idea of owning real estate. In the beginning we had so many questions. Today, we are so well acquainted with Jeva's management style, it is rare that we ever have a question that we don't already know the answer to," said Henry.

Partnering with Others

I asked, "Why didn't you and Barbara just buy property on your own?"

Henry says, "I look at it this way. You must not only consider the return on your *investment dollars,* but also the return on your *time.* I cannot know every aspect of leasing, maintenance, financing, accounting, and marketing. If I owned an apartment building and ran into a specific problem, my lack of knowledge on a simple matter could prove to be very costly. But with several members, we are able to draw on the diverse expertise and skills of everyone in the group."

"Also, the economies of scale are important. If I own a 4-family building and 2 of my tenants move out, then I have quickly gone from being 100% occupied to being 50% vacant. When you are part of a group who owns, altogether, dozens or hundreds of apartments, you are not as susceptible to those wild swings. And, you have better buying leverage with vendors, and borrowing power with lenders. Also, having a team of partners is better when making decisions of where to buy and what type of property to invest in."

A Matter of Trust

But Henry stipulates that it all comes down to a matter of trust. He appreciates how discerning Jeva and Bobby were before approaching them to join in as real estate partners, and that has given them the confidence of knowing that all of the other partners, many of whom are good friends, were similarly selected.

"It is all about having a relationship built on trust," says Henry. "It doesn't mean that there is never any risk, or that there is never a potential for disagreements. But, having friends as my partners is the strongest type of security. Of course, I am always copied on the documentation, and I always review it. But, that is just added security on top of the relationships. Otherwise, I would be left to rely solely on the documentation. I'm not a lawyer! If something goes wrong, I don't want to rely on a piece of paper! I want to rely on my relationships and my friendships."

Henry also believes that a partnership becomes stronger, if the members share similar goals and have the same perspective on life. He says, "Financial strength is secondary to perspective strength. It is great if everyone has similar financial strength, but it is more important to have a shared vision of the goals you want to achieve."

Okay, Henry. *Now* can I ask you about those hobbies and interests?

Partner Profile

Daniel Sui and Feng Xu

Across the Globe

Years ago, when I was in school, it seemed to me that Geography was all about memorizing the names of the tallest peaks, longest rivers, and coldest climates. I remember that we learned a lot about deserts, lakes, and oceans; the equator and the polar cap. But, I have to admit that I never found the subject of *Geography* to be especially interesting. That is, until I met Professor Daniel Sui, the Current Chair of the Geography Department at The Ohio State University.

The Youngest of Four

Dianzhi (Dan) Sui, and his wife Feng Xu, were both born in Beijing, China. Each were the youngest of 4 children. Both Dan and Feng had parents who emphasized the importance of gaining a good education; advice that has served them well throughout their lives.

Feng grew up in a family with three older brothers. Her mother managed the home during the day, and her father was an architect who specialized in the construction of high-rise residential property.

Dan also grew up in a household of 3 older siblings. Dan's father, a self-educated man, was somewhat of a logistical genius. His job was to manage the efficiencies of operation for a major railroad company in China. It was fascinating work that focused on optimizing time and space throughout the process of delivering goods to the marketplace. It entailed creating a system that minimized delay and maximized volume at every turn. It involved the integration of human labor and sophisticated machinery. Dan's mother was a member of the support staff at the same company.

In retrospect, Dan's father made a lasting impression on Dan that continues to this day.

"When I was still in elementary school, my father would stress to me the importance of pursuing a quality education. Looking back, I can see why he planted those seeds in my mind, while I was still very young."

Taking this advice to heart, Dan become a National Merit Scholar at Peking University, and by 1989, he had obtained an undergraduate degree in Geography and a master's degree in Cartography and GI Science, with an emphasis on spatial analysis, remote sensing, and computer mapping.

Georgia on My Mind

At this time, the University of Georgia had a geography department that was considered to be one of the finest in the United States. Located in the small college town of Athens, Georgia, it was the perfect school for Dan to advance his studies. Over the next four years, Dan and Feng enjoyed the music, energy, and Southern charm of Athens. He graduated four years later, *not only with a diploma in hand!*

Dan recalls, "I will never forget carrying our newborn daughter into the graduation ceremony. It was a wonderful day."

The Lone Star State

Dan and Feng would spend the next 16 years of their life in College Station, Texas, home to Texas A&M, the 6th largest university in the country, with an enrollment of over 58,000 students. Dan launched his career as an assistant professor in 1993. He began climbing the academic ladder and was on track to attain the tenured status of a full professor with an endowed chair by 2001.

Dan reminisces about College Station with great affection.

"College Station was a relatively small, quiet town. It was a great place to raise a family. And, we were only 90 minutes away from Houston, a city with a rich culture. We would visit there on weekends for all of the restaurants, plays, and museums. Houston also has a great Chinatown neighborhood with wonderful Chinese cuisine. I remember how much my father liked to spend time with us there."

Feng, with her Chemistry background, soon became a research associate, in the field of Physiology and Pharmacology, at Texas A&M's College of Veterinary Medicine.

Time for One More Challenge

In their early 40s, it would have been very easy for the Suis to cruise through their comfortable careers in Texas and enjoy the success that had come from their hard work and preparation. But, they felt the need to re-challenge themselves. So, they decided to move to Columbus, Ohio in 2009 and become a part of The Ohio State University. And it became a family affair.

Dan was first recruited by The Ohio State University to serve as the director for the Center of Urban and Regional Analysis (CURA). He then was appointed to serve as the Chair of the Department of Geography at OSU—one of the finest in the country. Feng joined OSU's College of Veterinary Medicine, cited as one of the top 5 veterinary schools in America by *U.S. News and World Report.* And, their daughter, Alice, is a pre-med student in biology studying to be an optometrist. (She was there at her father's graduation, so I am sure she will insist that he attend her's!). Starting in the fall of 2015, Alice will pursue her doctor of optometry degree at the SUNY School of Optometry in New York City.

Serving Multiple Constituents

You can sense the joy and excitement that Dan has from chairing a department with a faculty, staff, and graduate students of over 100 people, plus an additional 350 undergraduate majors. He likes serving multiple constituents where he has the opportunity to set an agenda and a direction that helps others succeed.

Dan says, "It is not about power or control. It is about pursuing the common good. It is all about creating a structured environment that can support and motivate the professors and the students to fulfill their potential."

"It is interesting to observe the first-year graduate students. They are competitive and work very hard. The first year is when they learn how to deliver things on a deadline. And a certain amount of pressure is good. It helps them become more productive. On the other hand, it is not good for them to become *overly* stressed. It is important that they seek an appropriate level of stress; that they discover a proper balance."

Dan continues, "They have to work on their personal growth, and at the same time be able to integrate their skills with others when working in a group. I suppose that is the paradoxical nature of being human; being alone as an individual and being part of a larger group."

The Geography of Things!

The Ohio State University defines the study of Geography as: *The study of the Earth as the home of humanity.* The holistic nature of geography is why Dan considers it to be such a fascinating intellectual pursuit.

"It is one of the few disciplines in academia that has an emphasis on seeing the big picture," Dan says. "We study how natural systems and social systems are interacting with one another. We look at how they influence each other."

According to Dan, this is one of the best times in history to be able to combine geographical research with the recent explosion of new technology.

"Geographic Information System (GIS) technology and other powerful technologies have provided us with an incredibly rich source of data. For the first time ever, we are able to track individual events, such as natural disasters, weather phenomena, market innovations and medical breakthroughs, and connect those to individual behavioral patterns such as community organization, shopping habits, social trends, and health changes. We can do this around the clock, 24-7."

Dan points out the over-arching importance of geography on other disciplines of study.

"Now at OSU, Geography is part of the division of Social and Behavioral Science in the College of Arts and Sciences. But, it wasn't long ago that it was part of the College of Business, due to the enormous impact geography has on commerce and economies in every region of the world."

Joining the Bountiful Group

When I asked how the Suis came to join the Bountiful group of investors, I discovered that they are neighbors of the Chen family.

"They are a very friendly family and they gave us a warm welcome when we arrived in Columbus. We became instant friends and enjoy going on walks and spending time together. They introduced us to Jeva, Bobby and the rest of the group."

Having been in real estate for a long time, I thought that I had considered every possible reason for investing in real estate. But, Dan's reason for investing surprised me.

"*Symbolically*, when you invest in real estate in the city where you live, it gives you a stronger sense of community. And if you think about it, it is more than just symbolic. You are *literally* investing in your community. You are more a part of it."

He adds, "And, I believe that it is less risky than stocks or bonds, because it is *tangible*. It is *real*."

Dan and Feng like to walk, swim, watch movies, and travel to interesting parts of the world. The Suis also like to visit their homeland once or twice a year to visit family and friends.

Having had the opportunity to get to know Professor Sui over the years, and learning about his geographic journey through life, I told him what my *takeaway* was, from his story.

"You have taken so much after your father," I said. "He encouraged you to learn. And you ended up choosing a field that is related to what he did. He built systems to help connect people to, over, and around their environment. He had to be sensitive to the concerns of customers, workers, manufacturers, and travelers every day. There is a lot of social and mechanical engineering involved in both of your lines of work."

It is yet another lesson for me on how parents can be a great influence on their children, and how a great teacher can make a subject like geography come alive!

Partner Profile

Bing and Charlene Liang

There is Something Magnificent About It!

Bing and Charlene Liang enjoy listening to music, travelling, and working in the yard of their Westchester County home in New York. They have two sons, Jeremy and George. Charlene is in the field of dentistry, and Bing owns an environmental consulting business.

Niche Analysis, Inc. is a successful company that tests and monitors water, air, gas, building materials, and soil for various pollutants and hazards such as asbestos, PCBs, mercury, mold, and lead.

It was an easy road to bountiful for the Liangs. It only took 30 years of arduous work, incredible risk, and overcoming what, to me, seems like unimaginable challenges. How difficult could that be?

I am always humbled by individuals who rely on their own entrepreneurial efforts to make a better life for themselves and their family. A couple of years ago, I wrote a book on the leadership skills of President Ronald Reagan. About these efforts he said, *there is something truly magnificent about it.*

This story is largely about the starting of a business. But first, some background.

Bing was born northwest of Beijing, the eldest of four children. After graduating as a medical student, Bing taught for three years at the same college he had attended. One day, Bing brought a colleague, who was in need of medical attention, to the hospital. It was there where Bing met Charlene, who worked as a doctor. Bing and Charlene were married in 1985, shortly before Bing left for the United States to further his education.

2 Fives, a Twenty, and a New Language to Learn

When Bing Liang arrived in America, he did not speak any English.

Not a single word.

He had $30.00 in his pocket.

He was in New York City.

Bing recalls that those first few days were very depressing. "I rented a bed in Chinatown that rented out for eight dollars per day, mostly to drug dealers and to people who were relatively homeless. I had come from a very poor area of China, but it was very nice and very clean. This place was the opposite of that."

After a few days, Bing moved into a basement apartment in Flushing, Queens, before relocating to the Bronx. There, he shared a room with a fellow student who could speak *some* English, but who was always at work or school. To learn the language, Bing had to enroll in English classes, and was given a tape player from a friend at church that also helped with the process.

"My great uncle paid for my first semester at NYU," recalls Bing. "I had never met him before, but we became very close. After that first semester, I was responsible for supporting myself and paying the tuition, which I remember was $2,800 per semester."

Bing went to school in the morning and worked for a restaurant at night. After a couple of years, Bing was fluent in English and transferred to Hunter College, where he studied Environmental Science. While in school, he took a job in the field, with JLC Environmental Consultants, which is where he began his career.

"It is interesting that you ask me about that first job, Garry. Because, just yesterday, I saw the owner of that company at a St. Patrick's Day party. Her name is Jennifer Lynn Carey. She is the *JLC.* She is a very good lady. I worked there for ten years. She was new to the business at the time and we were all learning together. It was a particularly hot industry in those years, especially dealing with asbestos-related issues. She started a good lab, went from Brooklyn to Manhattan, and expanded her company by hiring salespeople and a director of operations," says Bing.

Growing a Business

Bing decided to leave JLC to avoid the long commute back and forth from work, so he accepted a job offer where he would be closer to Westchester. But it was a huge company with a highly structured bureaucracy, and Bing did not have free reign to make important decisions, like he had in his previous job.

"I knew I wanted to operate my own business," recalls Bing. "But it seemed like such a daunting proposition, to start out brand new, so I purchased an existing business. In retrospect, it was a mistake. I might have well just started from scratch."

Bing says, "Business is very personal. So, when the previous owner left, so went his connections and relationships. After that first contract expired, I had to start developing my own client base. That first year or two, I wasn't able to draw a salary for myself."

After a while, however, Bing learned how to bid successfully for several city contracts. The profit margin on public work was extremely low, but it created a payroll base for the team of professionals he had assembled, and he was able to obtain larger contracts in both the public and private sectors.

"The difficult part of running your own business is setting goals in an industry that has so many market fluctuations and legislative changes. With a large staff, you are always juggling with different types of personalities, and we are always careful to adhere to the strict regulations inherent with our job," Bing says.

He continues, "But I like the creative process. It matches well with my personality; to improve the company and to improve myself. I think it is difficult for people to be happy if they are working for a big company that doesn't include them in that creative process."

Lessons from Their First Apartment

Bing and Charlene's first real estate investment was an apartment they bought in 1990 that faced the Hudson River and was within walking distance of the train station. They then bought a property and tore down the existing structure to build a new home.

"Through my work, I had become very familiar with different contractors, which gave me the confidence to construct our own home," Bing says.

However, because the real estate market for selling apartments was down, Bing and Charlene decided to rent the apartment, until the market rebounded. The timing of the real estate market forced them to become landlords. They learned two lessons from this experience.

Lesson #1: "We learned that if you hold apartments for a long enough period of time, it will eventually overcome dips in the market and appreciate in value. We ended up selling the property for 50% more than what we paid for it."

Lesson #2: "We discovered the importance of having good tenants, and taking the time to qualify prospective renters."

"Our first tenant was the perfect renter. He was a very nice man from Germany who always paid his rent on time, kept the property in perfect condition, and stayed there for five years. We expected all future tenants would be like that," says Bing.

Instead, the new tenant was terrible. "Basically, he ended up staying there for 5 months free, before we were able to evict him. And, he left the apartment in terrible condition."

However, the appreciated value of the investment came in handy when they sold the property and applied the proceeds towards Bing's company.

Paving Roads to Bountiful

Bing and Charlene like being *bountiful partners.* "We have made a lot of good friends through the partnership. We like the team concept, and when you find a good group, you want to stick with it. And we like the steady income from investing in real estate. It is certainly more predictable than the income derived from owning a service company."

Along the way, Bing was able to pave a smoother road for his younger brother, Chee, when he arrived in New York. The next *bountiful profile* will explain why Chee says that, "Bing was the most influential person in my life."

Learning more about how Bing was able to create a small business only adds to the respect and awe I have for entrepreneurs who are able to meet the challenges they face every day in the marketplace, make payroll for their staff, and provide for their families. There is something magnificent about it!

Partner Profile

Chee and May Liang

Intersections!

Chee and May Liang enjoy a productive and peaceful life in New York, surrounded by wonderful family and good friends. They both have careers they enjoy, their children attend outstanding schools, and they maintain a very busy and fruitful schedule.

On weekends, Chee finds time to fish the beautiful lakes of Westchester County, or watch a Yankees or Knicks game. And, he enjoys staying in physical shape by visiting the neighborhood fitness club. Chee likes to be outdoors, following in the tradition of his 82-year old father who has been an avid planter and gardener his entire life. Chee likes to work with his hands. He nurtures the vegetable garden in their backyard, which is full of fruit trees. His wife, May, enjoys picking vegetables and fruits when they are ready. She also loves cooking and baking meals for her family.

The Liang family enjoys a wonderful lifestyle that is full of satisfying work and activity. But, that was not always the case...

Over twenty years ago, Chee, a textile engineer with a bachelor's degree from Northern China, arrived in the bustling metropolis of New York City with $50 dollars in his pocket and ideas to get better and higher education.

"My English was limited and I needed to improve my English before I could enroll in college level classes. At the same time, I needed to support myself," Chee says.

Dodging Cabs in Manhattan

Just a few days after arriving in New York, Chee was riding his bike through the busy traffic of Upper West Manhattan, delivering lunch meals to a company located in one of the skyscrapers that surrounded him. As he approached a crowded intersection, seemingly out of nowhere, a yellow cab darted through the light. While dodging the oncoming car, Chee flew off his bike, landing in the middle of the street.

"Here I was, in the middle of the street, food thrown everywhere, knowing that I could have been seriously injured. It was all very discouraging. I was thinking to myself, 'Why am I doing this?' It was not as if I didn't have a good education and opportunities back home in China. But, here I was, doing all of this for minimum wage and tips!"

Chee was very frustrated. However, he knew that his goal was to one day work in one of those skyscrapers.

Three Hundred Dollars, a Goal, and a Big Brother

Meanwhile, May found herself in a similar situation. Coming from relatively humble beginnings, May arrived in New York City with $300 and a goal to obtain a quality education.

May says, "Today, Chinese students are very affluent. But, back in the late 80s it was more of a struggle."

Fortunately for May, her brother had arrived two years earlier on an exchange scholarship, and he was a big help to her.

Together, they rented an apartment. Chee also relied on the help of an older brother.

Chee says, "My brother, Bing, was the most influential person in my life. He supplied me with a great foundation, financially arranged for everything, and helped me enroll in college. It was Bing who recommended that I switch from textile engineering to computer science, which has always provided great opportunities for me." To this day, Chee and May are very close with their brothers, and their families regularly spend time with each other.

Chee and May worked by day, and attended Hunter College at night.

May recalls, "At the time, things certainly seemed difficult. We were in a large metropolitan city, working and studying seven days a week. There was no break at all. Looking back, I would not say that these were particularly happy days, but we were hopeful! We knew that once we got our education and graduated, that we could change our lives dramatically."

After obtaining a master's degree in computer science, in 1991, Chee set out on his career.

Getting 'In the Door'

"I will never forget the day of my first interview," Chee says. "It was the same day May entered the hospital to have our first baby!" Chee was surprised that his first job actually ended up being in the field of medical testing.

"It was a lower paying job, but it got me in the door. From there I was able to advance into a position that consisted of one-half engineering and one-half information technology." This led to his work in network administration and, eventually, to his current position as Director of Infrastructure Services for an international company with over 160 branches along the east coast.

Chee says, "It has been my experience that, if you work hard, respect others, and are willing to learn, you will always have good opportunities."

After their first baby was born, May stayed home to take care of the family, and she wanted to prepare for a change in her career. She decided to earn an associate's degree at the Fashion Institute of Technology to work as a pattern maker, but that created problems with her back. She also recognized that her strengths were much more suited for the field of accounting, where she could apply the accounting degree she earned in China. For the past decade, she has spent her career as a payroll supervisor with a private, mid-sized software company, where she enjoys dealing effectively with any day-to-day challenges that arise.

Making Friends at Hunter College

It was at Hunter College, where Chee and May met Jeva Lin.

May smiles as she reminisces back to that time. "Jeva and I are both from the same city in South China, so we quickly became close friends. It always fascinated me that Jeva had such a big plan for her life. We were young students and our first thought was to just make sure we could pay the rent; to just survive! One day, when Jeva and I were walking through Brooklyn, we walked past this very old, very impressive house. Jeva looked up at it and said, 'One day I will *buy* that house! She always had a big vision for her future."

During that time together, Chee, May, and Jeva made a lot of friends. According to May, "Jeva has always taken great care to maintain those relationships, which is not always easy to do. She has always made it a priority to keep in touch with everyone. And, Jeva and Chee would often communicate back and forth to share their IT expertise with each other."

Cultivating an Interest in Real Estate

It was during a trip to visit Jeva in Columbus in 2009, that the Liangs became interested in real estate. Initially, they were surprised by the 96-unit apartment community that Jeva owned and operated.

"Coming from New York, we expected to see an apartment building that was several stories high," says Chee. Because of the lower land costs in Columbus, apartments are usually built at a low density ratio of 12 apartments per acre.

According to Chee, "We saw Jeva's records, balance sheets; how she runs her business. We were impressed, but still reluctant to invest. We knew we had to fund upcoming college costs for the kids and we didn't want to deplete a large portion of our savings. But, Jeva was very confident in the potential of Waterford Pointe Apartments, a large property that she and Bobby wanted to acquire. So, she offered us a preferred rate of return which we felt added a certain degree of safety for our investment."

It has been said that success is where opportunity meets preparedness. In this instance, the Liangs believed that this was a good opportunity because Jeva had the experience and energy to effectively manage the apartments. And the Liangs were prepared.

Chee recalls, "We were liquid. We had equity in our house and money in our savings account. And in Columbus we were able to invest in multiple units. With the high cost of real estate in New York, I doubt we could have afforded more than a well-located single family home. We were attracted to real estate because we like tangible things, and the physical condition of the apartments was very good," Chee says.

May adds, "It was important that we were good friends with Jeva first, and knew we could trust each other, and *then* good business partners...not the other way around."

Chee and May became the first people to invest with Spring Property Management.

Chee and May still miss their hometown and they plan to travel back to China often, when they retire. In the meantime, they enjoy watching their family grow. Their daughter, who has been greatly influenced by her relationship with her grandmother who is a retired schoolteacher, will soon get her degree in education. She enjoys playing the piano and likes to volunteer for various charitable projects in her spare time. Their son is enjoying his high school years and shares Chee's passion for sports. Together, the Liang family spends time on the weekends at their local Chinese school.

Through perseverance, an emphasis on higher education, and hard work, the travels of Chee and May Liang have found a road to bountiful, far beyond that crowded Manhattan intersection where a guy on a bicycle dodged a yellow cab.

Partner Profile

Dr. Feng and Ruju Chen

In *Key* with Each Other

I was honored to be invited by Jeva and Bobby to Spring Property Management's Annual Dinner, attended by the partners of their real estate group, Bountiful Investments. It was a great pleasure to spend time with so many people whom I have come to know over the months and years, as we all enjoyed a delicious meal of abalone, fresh fish, and other authentic Chinese cuisine. It was a very special occasion filled with great conversation, laughter, and singing.

Seated at a separate table, were all of their children, who were very friendly and polite as they shared in the meal and enjoyed each other's company. It is always heartening to hear how accomplished these kids are in their academics and in their extracurricular activities. My wife, Sherri, and I have always been impressed too by another common thread they seem to share with one another; a love for music.

This is certainly the case with the Chen family. Between Dr. Fred and Rudi Chen, and their two daughters, Lucy and Emily, they enjoy piano, violin, ballet, and singing. I guess you could say, as a family, they are hitting on all of the right notes!

Interpreting Opportunities

In the mid-1980s, Drs. Fred and Rudi Chen were attending physicians, practicing and teaching internal medicine at a prestigious medical school in Central China. Dr. Chen served as an interpreter for the Dean of the medical school, who was leading a large delegation from The Ohio State University (OSU). The trip was a part of a friendship visit between the State of Ohio and Hubei Province in 1987, which resulted in establishing a scholarly exchange between the two medical schools.

"That was back in the 80s," says Dr. Chen, "and to this very day, those two cities still maintain a great relationship with each other."

Dr. Chen was invited to become a visiting scholar at the OSU Medical School, where he published several papers in Neuroendocrinology, and completed his postdoctoral training as part of a research group. Dr. Chen passed two medical license examinations and began his residency training in the hospital, often working 80 to 100 hours per week.

Today, as board-certified doctor in Internal Medicine, Dr. Chen practices in the largest physician group in Central Ohio, and is an active member of the Board of Directors that oversees the activity of 280 physician members.

Rudi Chen arrived in the United States in May of 1990, 8 months after her husband came to Columbus. Over the last 24 years, she has been involved in basic biomedical science research at the Nationwide Children's Hospital Research Institute. She has participated in projects of advancing research on the adenovirus/HIV vaccine, neonatal necrotizing enterocolitis, and liver fibrosis.

According to Rudi Chen, "We both feel very fortunate to be part of a profession where we can help people."

The couple are proud of their lovely daughters, Lucy and Emily.

Lucy has followed in the medical footsteps of her parents. An exceptional student, she earned her medical degree from the Icahn School of Medicine at Mount Sinai, in New York City and was honored as a member of Alpha Omega Alpha Honor Society for her outstanding academic skills. Currently, she is in her second year of Dermatology. Emily is a junior in high school, and her current interests are less related to the field of medicine. Emily enjoys swimming, photography, and, as a past member of the Columbus Children's Choir, singing. Both sister share a love for tennis and music.

Fulfilling Dreams

According to Fred and Rudi Chen, "We share the same American dream with all immigrants from all over the world. Over the last 25 years we have worked hard, and we feel very fortunate to be in the medical health profession where we can help serve other people. We also feel fortunate in being able to participate in a group of dedicated business partners, led by Bobby and Jeva."

One of Dr. Chen's friends encouraged the Chens to consider investing in the real estate business.

Dr. Chen says, "My friend pointed out that the recession had made it much more difficult for people to afford a house, which increased the demand for rental property."

"People always need a place to live, whether it be buying a house or renting an apartment," says Dr. Chen. "After 2008, the lending requirements for buying a home became more stringent, and buyers had to make larger down payments. At the same time interest rates for investors began to fall. All of these factors combined to create good opportunities for investors. We thought it was worthwhile to take advantage of those market conditions."

Rudi Chen added, "Mutual funds can be good investments, but they are not always safe, and can drop sharply in value. Owning real estate has resulted in stable returns and good tax advantages."

Most investors of multifamily property have no interest in performing day-to-day property management, and the Chens are no exception.

As the couple explain, "Frank introduced us to this investors group. Along with the other investors, we trust the management team. We enjoy the frequent communications and annual investor meetings to update the status of investment and to discuss new plans. The group investment also allows us to focus on our active life of travel, gardening, cooking, daily exercise, friend gatherings, and various community activities."

Maintaining an active life is an essential ingredient to enjoying good health. Dr. Chen enjoys sharing this philosophy with his patients.

Stay Healthy …
Because Your Life is Worth a Million!

Dr. Chen says, "I like to help my patients be aware of how important their health is, not just to them, but to so many others. Sometimes I will take out a pen and a piece of paper and say it this way: 'You are number 1 in your life'"

Dr Chen then writes down the number 1 on the paper.

And then he starts adding zeros!

"I add zeros for each of the important people in their life; their spouse, their children, their parents, their friends. Once I get to six zeros, I explain that their life is worth a million! And to make the most of their life they need to stay as healthy as possible, not only for themselves, but for the others who depend on them. It helps my patients to think outside of themselves, and to consider how their health impacts others."

Since I began this story on a musical note, I am hoping that you, the reader, will allow me to end this story on a harmonious pun. You see, my wife and I also like music and play the piano. So, I guess you could say that Dr. Chen's perspective on health, really struck a *chord* with us, seemingly hitting on all the right *keys*! But with puns like that, I am wondering if we will be invited back to next year's dinner!

Partner Profile

Sheri Hsueh

Investing in People

Watching the dim sky through the airplane window, Sheri, a young lady in 1985, decided she would stay overnight at the airport in Salt Lake City. This was her first night in the United States. The original plan had been to meet with Dr. William, the Dean of Graduate Studies, in his office at The University of Utah. However, the flight had been delayed several hours, due to snow.

She only had forty dollars with her, and as she explains, "It would not be enough for a trip by taxi and one night at a hotel. Plus, at such a late hour, it might not be even possible to find anyone in the department to help me."

As she walked out wearily from the plane, she was pleasantly surprised to find that Dr. William was waiting for her, along with two other Chinese students outside the gate.

Sheri had a cozy night in a neat room at the dorm. The daily room rate of $13.90 cautioned her against spending any of her $40.00 on food. On day two, however, she walked into a fast food restaurant and saw a meal that was priced at 459. She did not order the meal, however, because there was no decimal point applied to the number, so there was no way of being certain that the price was $4.59, and not $45.90. (Other *bountiful partners* tell me that they too had experiences very similar to this.)

On the third morning, Sheri awoke, feeling as though there were numerous fireflies around her. When they all disappeared, as she tried to capture one, she realized that she was just 'seeing stars', the effect of not having eaten much food during those first three days.

Very soon, Sheri found new friends, and through Professor Bean, she was able to receive her first pay check of $100 in advance for her research assistantship. The opportunity to work as a research assistant gave her a smooth start with her graduate study at the University of Utah, and later on led her to pursue her PhD degree at the University of Chicago. This dramatically changed her future life.

A Shift in Focus

Over the past twenty years, Sheri's positions with multinational banks have taken her to dozens of different countries where she works on business intelligence, market analysis, data mining and risk modeling.

For a long while, Sheri's entire focus was on work and accomplishment.

"I was definitely a workaholic," She says. "It wasn't unusual for me to work through entire nights. I remember one day in particular when I worked 24 straight hours, without leaving my desk"

All the hard work and countless hours of determination paid off for Sheri. She accomplished a lot, and her innovative solutions in data-mart, business intelligence and CRM architecture brought her many successes. One day, after a significant accomplishment, a big question appeared in her mind: "So what?"

Over time, she continued to ask herself this same question. Finally, after her many years of experience, she came to the realization that it was a lot more meaningful to put effort in *developing people* than simply in getting the job done.

This change in focus, from *work projects* to *people*, was initially inspired by Sheri's experiences with her son, Kye, "the only boy God gave us." Tragically, her husband was diagnosed with cancer when Kye reached 4, and he had to undergo several surgeries. During this time, Sheri gave as much love, time and energy as she could to Kye, to make sure that he received no less love than other children. "The experiences we shared together were truly rewarding," Sheri says with a delightful smile.

"These experiences taught me that when one invests one's time in a *person*, it is more sustainable and meaningful. Accomplishments at work can often be disrupted by future technologies, market changes or situation changes. To some extent, the passion to work sometimes made me feel as if I were building sand castles."

"It is much more meaningful to invest in people; to help in their development so that they are prepared for anything that occurs in the future. When developing my team became my priority, my work became more significant and enjoyable."

A Blessed Family and Friendship

Born in Tianjin, a city about ninety miles from Beijing, Sheri was the seventh of nine siblings. Her parents and grandparents were highly educated. Her father was a professor in the field of finance and economics, and her mother attended college as a medical student before becoming a homemaker to the big family. Sheri was very close to her grandfather and her grandmother who was the only female dean in the most famous high school in Tianjin.

After junior high school, Sheri did not attend high school.

She started to work in a ball-bearing production factory. "I would have worked my entire life as a factory worker, had my father not taught me English." Sheri's father was a graduate of St. John's University in Shanghai, and was a wonderful teacher. Another *Bountiful Partner*, Frank Wong, was one of his students.

In 1977, after a 10 year hiatus, the college entrance examination system was resumed. Sheri was among the first wave of college students, after the Cultural Revolution. During her first summer in college, she worked outdoors, digging up river silt and moving bricks for one Yuan per day (about 33 cents). With her father's help, Sheri was able to make a living by teaching professional English in the summer of the following year.

Having grown up in a family full of love and care, Sheri naturally developed a trusting personality. Through Frank's introduction, Sheri joined the real estate partnership that purchased Waterford Point Apartments. She trusted Jeva and Bobby because she trusted Frank. When she met the couple for the first time, the trust became real and vivid. "They were brilliant, professional, and trustworthy friends. I was totally impressed." This motivated Sheri to join what she refers to as, "the adventurous journey, *walking to Bountiful*."

She recalls, "I thought the *property* was a good investment. However, as a risk manager, I really believe that risk lies in trusting the *people* in the deal."

Sheri's perspective on real estate is unique. "Buying real estate is like creating a piece of art. So many things have to come together for it to turn out well."

A Bountiful Experience

As my meeting with Sheri, to discuss this book, was winding down, she shared with me a shocking experience. A couple of years ago, she nearly accidentally killed herself on a freeway. This happened one day, after getting off a plane after flying for thirteen hours. Having helped Kye settle down at his summer camp at Stanford University, she took a short nap for 20 minutes and then got back on the freeway and was travelling at the 70 mph speed limit on a curved road.

For several seconds she was unaware of anything. Maybe she dozed off, or maybe she was heavily daydreaming. Whatever the case, the moment she 'woke up', she found herself driving on the emergency road, hurtling towards the freeway barrier. It would have been a tragic ending, had she not become alert at just that exact time.

Afterwards, others attributed her good fortune to luck. Sheri, though, has a different perspective. She told me that the very first thing she saw when she returned home was a television report of a terrible crash, *exactly* like the one she had just avoided.

"I was totally shocked. I believe that God was telling me that it was Him who saved me. I will never forget that day." Then, Sheri began an interesting discussion on the meaning of life, wealth, and time. I asked Sheri what was the main lesson she had learned from her varied experiences.

"I'm not sure what the purpose of your book is, Garry, but the most important life lesson I could share with you is not specifically about success or real estate."

Well, what is it then?

She looked at me thoughtfully, and firmly said, "Through Jesus alone, and in my walk with Him, is the road toward a bountiful life."

Partner Profile

Gary and Lisa Lee

I Want to Tell You About a Slow Boat from China

It was a very cold morning in March of 2013, when Lisa Yee flew to New York with Jeva Lin for a busy and exciting day.

"Jeva had just signed a contract on behalf of some of the *bountiful partners* to purchase a townhouse building in Manhattan, consisting of 20 apartments. As part of her due diligence, she had arranged for a full day of meetings. Everything was very fast-paced and organized," Lisa recalls.

With logistical help from fellow bountiful partners, Chee Liang, and Kerri Zou, Jeva and Lisa travelled via taxis, subways, Uber cars, and good old-fashioned walking.

First, it was to the seller's home in Short Hills, New Jersey, to learn more history about the subject property. Then, onto City Diner at 90th and Broadway to hear the property manager's assessment of the condition of the property, the tenant profile, and the engineering report.

After that, was an important meeting at 1 Battery Park Plaza with a potential lender, who presented a quote sheet with corresponding expense figures, at the low interest rate of 2.85%.

From there, they travelled to East 73rd Street for a quick *walkthrough* of the property with the listing broker.

Their final appointment of the day was at Times Square to meet with their attorney who was coordinating the closing.

Lisa remembers. "Afterwards, we had dinner and went to a ballet show at the Lincoln Center. The entire day was a great experience!"

Lisa Yee has had many great experiences. One of them was the day she married Gary Yee, her husband of 33 years. It was an international wedding. Gary became the first American Born Chinese (ABC), from Columbus, Ohio, to bring a wife from China to America.

What Led Up To the Wedding?

Gary's grandparents lived in Detroit, Michigan where they owned and operated a laundry service. In 1923 they had a son, Arthur Yee, Gary's grandfather.

Shortly after the American Stock Market Crash of 1929, The Yees returned to China. Several years later, at the outbreak of World War II, Arthur spent 50 days aboard what can only be described as a slow boat from China, to return to America where he volunteered to serve in the U.S. Navy.

When the war ended, Arthur settled in Columbus, Ohio, with his wife, Pui Yee. He went to work as a seafood chef at the Jai Lai Restaurant, which was a very popular dining spot, known for their steaks and fish.

The Opening of Art & Pui's

In 1972, Arthur Yee ventured out to open his own restaurant at *The French Market*, billed as Columbus's original lifestyle center, featuring European-inspired architecture with outdoor shopping, apartments, and entertainment venues. Incorporating his name with his wife's name, he called the restaurant Art & Pui's.

It became a family affair. Gary and his four younger sisters worked there day and night.

Gary recalls, "There were very few Chinese restaurants back then. We were located in the food court—one of the first indoor food courts in the country. Busses full of tourists from all over the Midwest would unload shoppers and diners wanting to see what *The French Market* looked like."

"Everything we served was made from scratch, and we were very successful," Gary says.

The single drawback was the long hours that were needed to run a restaurant.

"We worked 10 hours each day, 7 days a week. And, we never took vacations. But, for me, the best part was meeting with and developing relationships with so many of the people. I really liked that part. It fits with my personality," Gary says.

An International Marriage

During this time, a former classmate of Gary's mother, told her about a young lady from the city of Taishan, in Guangdong Province. Her name was Lisa. She was the eldest of four children, and had just finished two years of college, preparing to become a teacher. Consistent with local Chinese custom of that day, Gary and Lisa were married, and then began dating.

"I will never forget my first day in the U.S.," Lisa says. "It was Arthur Yee's 60th birthday." (13 years later, on that same date, their daughter, Eileen, would be born.)

When Arthur sold his restaurant in 1986 and retired, Gary opened *his* first restaurant, *China Express,* and soon thereafter, a second one.

"We held to the motto that the customer was always right," says Gary. "We always tried our best to accommodate our patrons. Our business did very well, and it was something that I always enjoyed."

A Growing Family

With three children—Brandon, Kane, and Eileen—Lisa became concerned that the long hours at the restaurant were taking too much of a toll on the family.

"I took Eileen to work with me every day, but I just felt that I needed to concentrate more on her. So, I went to work for an accounting firm that offered me flexible hours," says Lisa.

A New Business

After 11 years with the accounting firm, Lisa took the risky step of branching out on her own to create a new business. From a conversation she had with her sister, a chemical engineer, who was lamenting the high costs of disposing waste products into landfills, Lisa devised new ways to recycle products; ways that were more cost effective and better for the environment. It is a green initiative that has provided Gary and Lisa with a platform to meet people, travel the world, and give back to poor communities.

"One thing we are very excited about," says Lisa, "is a water filtration system that we were able to donate to a village in China. It provides 35 families with cleaner water, free of chemical pollutants that travel downstream."

An Unexpected Addition to the Yee Clan

On a sad day in 2010, Gary and Lisa experienced the passing of a very close friend, which left her 10-year-old son, Steve, without a home. Once again, the Yees found themselves in a position to be of help. They adopted Steve, who became part of their family.

I wanted to know where this theme of helping others came from. I asked Lisa, "Who was one of your favorite mentors in life, and what is the best advice you have received over the years?"

"My aunt, Pauline Yee, was a wonderful mentor to Gary and me. She was the personal secretary for Ohio Governor James Rhodes for more than 30 years. She had a good heart and was always helping people. She was a responsible saver of money, and was a very polite person. We learned from her the importance of surrounding yourself with good people, and of being loyal to friends and family."

Old Cars, Books, and Manhattan Townhomes

Today, their oldest son, Brandon is a chemical engineer with an RN license, Kane just finished college with a degree in business, and Eileen, who enjoys playing the flute, cello, and violin, is in her first year of college pursuing a degree in international business. And, Steve is enjoying his high school years.

In their free time Gary enjoys going to auctions for antiques and old cars, travelling, and listening to rock 'n' roll music from the 60s. Lisa likes reading fictional books and books related to business and success, while listening to classical or country music. They both spend time at the Ohio Chinese School and provide the food for many of the school events. They also look forward to the Yee family's annual reunion picnic, which is where they originally met Jeva Lin and Bobby Yu.

Reflecting back on that cold March day in Manhattan, Lisa says, "For twenty years, Gary and I wanted to buy real estate in New York. When I heard that Jeva was looking there, I told her we wanted to be included! For us, joining a successful group was better than going on our own. It's less money and we can piggyback on their experience."

Lisa says, "Real estate offers leverage, is tangible, and has good tax benefits. The stock market can go down. I remember the huge negative impact the dot com bust made. It takes a long time to rebound from that."

Her thought on the stock market took me back to the crash of '29 that prompted Gary's grandparents to travel back to China, and his father's 50 day voyage back to America that started it all … on a slow boat from China.

Partner Profile

Chenny Zhao and Mei Hong

The Road from Shanghai

Today, Chenny Zhao and Mei Hong enjoy spending time with friends over a cup of tea. Chenny likes watching World Cup Soccer matches and Mei enjoys trying out new restaurants. Both of them like to travel.

"Preferably we like to visit warmer climates," says Mei. "But my dream trip is to travel through Europe someday."

They spend most of their free time, however, at the Chinese Christian Church, where Chenny is a Church Deacon, involved in their Community Outreach program. Since arriving in Columbus 16 years ago, they have participated in bible studies, worship services, and fellowship meetings at the church.

They have two sons. Kelvin is taking pre-med classes at Kent State University and enjoys playing soccer and piano. Christopher is in 8th grade, plays piano and guitar, and runs cross-country.

"We have always tried to encourage our kids to establish strong friendships at Church. It is so important for them to be in a group of friends that can help each other lead positive lives," Mei says.

The Road from Shanghai

Mei Hong and her three younger brothers are from the province of Jiangxi, in Mainland China. She recalls being a young student in the city of Yichun.

"Once a year, in the summer, everyone would take a college administration test that would determine your placement in college," recalls Mei. Her first day in class, she looked around the room at her fellow classmates. They all appeared to be quite a bit older that her. That is because Mei was only 14 years old when she entered college.

Mei took classes in education to become a teacher, which is exactly what she did for three years, before returning to college for a master's degree (and ultimately a PhD) in Computational Chemistry.

Chenny and his two younger brothers were born in Hunan Province, in the city of Shuangfeng. He was studying for his master's degree in Psychology, in Shanghai, one of the most populated cities in the world, with over 23 million inhabitants, when a friend of his introduced him to Mei. It is where Chenny and Mei got married.

Chenny recalls, "We enjoyed living in Shanghai. There are a lot of economic opportunities there, and the school system is outstanding (there are over 30 universities and colleges in the city)."

Shanghai is a very popular tourist destination because of their museums, arts, and fashion. Mei remembers, "One of the things I enjoyed most was window shopping! I couldn't *buy* anything, but I liked to *see* all of the new designs."

Finding an affordable apartment in Shanghai was virtually impossible for the newlyweds. So, they lived in dormitory-style accommodations as Chenny prepared to take the entrance exam for admittance into American universities.

"When President Reagan visited China, it really marked a turning point in relations between China and the United States," Mei recalls.

A Heartbreaking Decision

When both Chenny and Mei were accepted to the University of Louisville in Kentucky, they were forced to make one of the most difficult decisions of their lives.

The risks involved with immediately bringing their infant son, Kelvin, along with them, as they navigated in a new country, with new jobs and demanding school schedules, was just too high. They decided to leave Kelvin in the good care of Mei's parents as they forged ahead to carve a future for their family. Within a couple of years, they had created an environment where the three of them could flourish together as they made a new life for themselves.

"We have so much regret with that decision," Mei says.

But, I wondered … what other alternative did they have? I asked, "I am trying to think what I would have done if the roles were reversed. If my wife and I had a great opportunity in China that would greatly impact us *and* our child, how could we not take advantage of that? And if we did, how could we *possibly* bring our child on day one? We wouldn't know the language, the customs, or the housing situation. We wouldn't really know who we could trust to watch over our child while we were at work and school."

I continued *thinking out loud.* "I could understand feeling remorse if your son was not left in good hands. But, in this case, you knew he would be well-cared for, by the same parents who raised you."

Mei responded, "It doesn't matter if it was a logical choice or not, Garry. Emotionally, it was heartbreaking until we were all reunited."

Chenny and Mei have fond memories of the southern charm and friendly culture of Louisville. They liked the architecture, the contoured landscape, and the Kentucky Derby.

But when they were offered great computer science jobs in Columbus, they moved.

"It is a great place to raise a family," Chenny says. "We like Columbus, because it is not too small, and not too big. It is not too slow, and not too fast."

A Funny Story

Mei laughs when she recalls a humorous event that happened shortly after being hired by MCI.

"I closed my office door without realizing that I had left my key inside. So, I knocked on the senior manager's door. He was a very nice person," Mei says. "I couldn't pronounce my 'l's very well at the time. So, when I told him that I had locked myself out, he became excited and said, 'You knocked yourself out!' "

Mei greatly enjoys her current position at Chase, where she analyzes data to make loss forecasts that determine reserve requirements, product pricing, etc. that adhere to all of the government regulations and banking laws.

"I love being part of important decisions that have a direct impact on long term and short term strategies. It is valuable work with practical application. The relationship with the team and fellow managers is very good," she says.

When Mei Met Jeva

Fellow *bountiful partner*, Jeva Lin, recalls meeting Mei for the first time. "My daughter, Gina, and her son, Kelvin, have been close friends from church since they were ten years old. I remember being so impressed when Mei organized a swimming program for the kids. She was very involved. You could tell that she wanted to help people. I *still* remember the flyer she put together to promote it!"

Mei recalls a gathering event that Jeva hosted for the kids at her house one day. "Afterwards, we were talking and Jeva mentioned that she was in the 'Dee Chang' business, which, in Chinese, means *real estate.* I thought she said 'Dee Tang', which means *carpet.* So I initially thought Jeva was in the carpet business!"

Eventually, Mei discovered the error, and when her brother wanted to invest in real estate, Mei went to Jeva for advice.

Focusing On Priorities

"We enjoy our time so much at work, church, and the Ohio Chinese School. Being part of the partnership allows us to focus on those things." Chenny says.

For instance, rather than despair over the amount of time the kids spend on video games, Mei re-channels their interest by teaching a class on how to create computer coding to make their own games.

"I show them that it is not just a way to play, but flip it around to make it a learning experience. They learn various computer languages, such as Scratch and Python. They have to employ logic and become creative," Mei says.

One student has actually announced his intention of making program design his career!

And, having firsthand experience with some of the dilemmas and challenges that face parents today, both Chenny and Mei created a parenting seminar that deals with emotional quotients, anger management issues, money management, and various ways mothers and fathers can become better parents.

On a recent medical mission trip to Nicaragua, Kelvin saw up-close why delivering good medical care serves such a great purpose. His experience further motivated him to continue his medical studies; studies made possible by his determination, and the determination of a pair of newlyweds, long ago, to discover for their family, a road to bountiful.

Partner Profile

Xiao Li and Hongying Zhang

Those Five Things

Today, Xiao Li and his wife, Hongying Zhang smile as they recall the five things they, and all of their friends, dreamed of owning when they were young. "We wanted a camera, a motorcycle, a microwave oven, a refrigerator, and a television! That was it! Those five things!"

Xiao Li and Hongying are from two beautiful parts of China. Xiao from the city of Wuxi, less than 100 miles from Shanghai, in the province of Jiangsu, and Hongying from Qichun, in Hubei. They met each other in the mid-80s at Wuhan University, where Xiao received his master's in Math and Hongying graduated with a degree in journalism.

They were married one month before Xiao left for America in 1988 with $200 dollars in his pocket, a scholarship to attend The Ohio State University, and the opportunity to earn $800 per month as a teacher's assistant.

"Dormitory accommodations were too expensive to afford, so I rented a one room apartment off-campus for $150.00 per month," recalls Xiao. "My intention was to further my education and earn some extra money before returning to China."

While Xiao could *read* English very well, he took English language classes to become proficient enough to *verbally* communicate in the classroom. He also began his studies in computer science.

A year passed before Hongying was able to follow her husband to Columbus. Her first impression of the city was "kind of depressing".

Home of the Buckeyes

"There were no mountains or lakes nearby. And, everything was so flat!" she recalls. Since then, she has come to appreciate Columbus as a good place to raise a family; a city with a high standard of living and good housing at affordable prices.

When Hongying explained how she had switched over from journalism to pursue her degree in computer science, I asked her, "Wasn't that extremely difficult to go from journalism to computer science? They are two very different fields of study."

Her husband answered my question. "It must not have been too difficult. She was the top student in her class every year!" he said

During those first few years, the couple rarely ate out or spent money on entertainment. Instead, they adhered to a very tight budget and focused on school and work. Hongying took a job as a waitress to help make ends meet.

Then, shortly after their first child, Amy, was born, Xiao began work as an outside consultant for CompuServe, which led to a fulltime position with the company.

A Booming Economy

It was a booming time in the computer industry as thousands of dot com companies were being created. It was the ground floor of the creation of the Internet, and Xiao and Hongying (who also went to work for CompuServe), were a part of it.

"It was a very exciting time," recalls Xiao. There was a high demand for IT professionals. The income was very good and the companies were big enough that there was plenty of opportunity for lateral moves to different departments and for job advancement. Everyone received regular salary increases and bonuses, and there were often competing offers from other companies."

CompuServe was then purchased by American Online (AOL), who immediately laid off a large percentage of their workforce. Fortunately, they provided very generous severance packages.

"It was great for me," laughs Hongying. "I had only been there three months, and they gave me a six-month severance package. I went out and bought a new Toyota Camry!" She later went to work as a software programmer at Sarcom, where she has been for the last 16 years.

For the remaining staff, AOL provided stock options.

Xiao recalls. "We came to expect the stock price to increase every day. If there was a day when the price did not increase by at least $2.00, we would look at each other and ask, 'What went wrong?'"

Internet Bubble

Then there came a *second* layoff. "When this happened," says Xiao, "the people who were let go redeemed their stock options. This turned out to be a very fortunate thing because the stock price at that time was extremely high."

Xiao was not laid off, but when he eventually redeemed his shares, the prices were still favorable. Not long thereafter, however, the bubble in the hi-tech stock market burst and the value of tech stocks plummeted.

That experience is one of the reasons Xiao and Hongying decided to invest in real estate.

A Shift to Real Estate

"I saw the crash of the tech market," says Xiao. "That made us skeptical enough to want to diversify into real estate. If the stocks crash again, the real estate will still be there. We have also met with various insurance reps to hear about their annuity programs, but we still think that real estate is a better choice for us."

However, Xiao insists that they have no interest in dealing with maintenance issues and the other day-to-day operations of owning real estate. He explains, "I am busy enough at work. I don't have time for that. Besides, I am not that handy. I can do a few things, but not like Bobby (Yu) can."

The couple's daughter, Amy, who was valedictorian of her high school class and is currently taking pre-med classes in college, is a good friend of Bobby and Jeva's daughter, Gina. The two girls met in the junior high school church program that was organized by Mai Hong (another *bountiful partner* profiled in this book). "That is how we became acquainted with Bobby and Jeva's real estate investments," says Hongying

A Change of Priorities

Their desire for 'those five things' has waned over the years.

Today, their priorities are focused on their work, travelling to China to visit their parents every year, and church activities.

"We do not have much leisure time. I tell people that I have become a cab driver for the kids!" laughs Hongying.

Xiao is a deacon at their church, where the entire family is very active. Xiao, Hongying, Amy, and their son, David, also enjoy various activities and programs that take place at the Ohio Chinese School.

So much better than those five things!

Partner Profile

Yicun Wu and Kerri Zou

A Family Affair

All of the success stories in *A Road to Bountiful* have a common theme; a shared thread that weaves through the lives of the *bountiful partners.* It is *family.* In case after case, story after story, the people featured in this book have both received help and given help to family members searching for their own road to bountiful. They search for a bountiful world of educational, spiritual, financial, and relational growth, complete with family and friends who look out for each other. This allegiance to family, this emphasis on giving each other a hand-up is well-illustrated by the following story of Yicun Wu and Kerri Zou, who reside in Great Falls, Virginia, near Washington, D.C.

Let's start with the Wu family. **Y** do you ask? Because **Y** icun has a brother, **Y** iding, and a sister, **Y** imao. All of them were born in China to Ningkun Wu and Yikai Li.

The Flying Tigers

An orphan as a child, Ningkun Wu was a self-taught man who became a translator for the U.S. Air Force during World

War II. In 1941, he was a translator with the Flying Tigers, the famous American Volunteer Group (AVG) that was first created to help defend China against Japanese forces just prior to America's entry into the war.

The Flying Tigers consisted of 3 fighter squadrons of top aces, including the legendary Gregory 'Pappy' Boyington. The pilots adopted a radically different approach to air combat that proved to be incredibly successful. The shark-faced nose art of their planes remains the most recognizable image of any combat aircraft of World War II.

After the war, Ningkun studied English Literature at the University of Chicago, and then returned to China because he wanted to be of help to his homeland. However, it was a time of great political turmoil, which resulted in unsteady employment for Ningkun and Yikai, both of whom were English teachers.

Lifting Each Other Up!

In 1980, Yiding moved to California where he enrolled in Stanford University. Yimao arrived a year later to attend the College of Notre Dame in the San Francisco Bay Area.

Yicun credits his older brother and sister for making his success possible. "When I first came to the U.S.," he says, "they helped me with tuition and provided a place for me to live. At first, school was very difficult for me, because plant pathology in this country was very different than what I was accustomed to. It was taught on a more *molecular* level. I lost interest and took odd jobs in construction to make ends meet. My brother and sister always encouraged me."

Yicun continues, "I started over; this time in computer science. I attended community college and then spent four years at Manchester College."

This path led Yicun to what he considers to be his true calling.

"Like both of my parents," says Yicun, "I can read very fast, and I really enjoy interpreting information."

So when he landed the position of patent examiner for the United States Patent and Trademark Office, in Washington, D.C., he found the perfect niche for himself, the perfect job.

"It is a fascinating field," says Yicun. "You must convert abstract ideas into literal interpretation. And you must also be able to take the literal and turn it into the abstract."

"For example, a patent lawyer might approach us with the broadest possible interpretation for a new invention that his client has created. It is up to us to determine the proper scope of that invention; to narrow the scope down to a legal description that deserves protection under the law."

"Conversely, sometimes a concept or idea with a seemingly narrow use can be expanded to include other abstract applications."

Lifting Each Other Up ... Again!

Years after Yicun had received so much advice and financial help from his older siblings, it was particularly gratifying for Yicun to be able to return the favor to his older brother, Yiding, who found himself without work after the tech bust began in 1999.

"I suggested that he too might enjoy the patent and trademark field, which led to a good position for him as a patent expert with a very good law firm," says Yicun.

Not surprisingly, Yiding and Yimao continue to keep a close relationship with their parents, Ningkun and Yikai, who moved to California in the early 90s to be nearer their children.

"I Wanted to See the World."

Kerri Zou learned English in China. "I was very fortunate to learn English in China from a young man from the United

States. It was a very rare opportunity for me, and he was a very good teacher. I was determined to go to the United States. I wanted to see the world!" Kerry recalls.

After graduating from college in China, Kerri received a full scholarship from Penn State University in 1989, where she followed her professor's advice to pursue a master's degree in chemistry. This led to a good job with Bristol-Myers Squibb, one of the world's leading pharmaceutical companies.

However, her younger brother, Kevin, helped her transition from the physical experimentation of pharmacy, to the theoretical chemistry of information technology.

A Younger Brother's Help

"My brother encouraged me to switch from pharmacology to IT, which I enjoy a lot more," says Kerri.

"In the IT world, I am able to do more thinking on paper. I prefer IT because working on formulaic calculations and coding allows me to be more creative. But I would never have been able to make that transition without my brother's assistance," she says.

Through a mutual friend, Kerri met Yicun. Two years later they were married. Kerri instantly liked the D.C. area.

"Washington has a great diversity of people, businesses, and professions," she says. "We really enjoy the cultural environment. There is a combination of great new things and wonderful museums."

An Irrational Decision that Led to a Bountiful Road

"In 1993 we bought our first house," recalls Kerri. "We couldn't afford much. So, we purchased a very small house in Washington, D.C. It was really an irrational decision, because when it came time to buy a larger home to accommodate our growing family, it was impossible to sell our old house quickly. We didn't have any time to wait, so we decided to rent it out."

Kerri enrolled in real estate classes to learn more about the intricacies of owning rental property. Over the next few years, that small house in D.C. increased dramatically in value to over four times what they had paid for it.

"When that happened," Yicun explains, "Kerri and I decided to refinance that original property. We took out an equity line-of-credit. This provided us with the downpayment to purchase six other homes."

Kerri also learned Spanish because this is the language of so many of their tenants.

"Owning real estate can be very stressful, especially in the beginning," she says. "There are the legal issues, and you have to collect the rent. It is a big risk. Will it go up or down in value? Will we be able to keep the property occupied?"

"But in retrospect, it has been a good decision for us. Over the long-term, it works very well," she says.

All Roads Lead to Family and Friends

Annie Pu (featured earlier in this book), was one of Yicun's fellow classmates at agricultural college in China. She introduced Yicun and Kerri to the group of *bountiful partners.*

Today Yicun and Kerri enjoy travelling with their daughters, Rachel and Michelle, to National Parks and walking around the Mall Area. Yicun likes going on long hikes, and Kerri enjoys her vegetable garden and has recently taken classes in Tai Chi.

Kerri's brother, and his wife, also have two daughters. They live only a few minutes away from Yicun and Kerri, as do Kerri's parents.

When I asked them to share advice from their experiences, their reply was very similar to the other *bountiful partners.* "Keep investing in your friends and family. You will always get something in return!"

Partner Profile

Chris Wang and Maggie Lin

Necessity is the Mother of Invention

***Necessity is the** mother of invention* is an old English proverb that suggests that challenging circumstances can inspire creation and discovery. This story is about travelling a bountiful road to real estate out of necessity.

1994 was an exciting year for experts in computer graphics with a Master's Degree in Communications Art from the New York Institute of Technology in Manhattan. The young graduates were some of the early pioneers in a world that was going digital. They were on the ground floor. Jeva Lin's sister, Maggie Lin, was such a person.

"While I was in school, I put together a portfolio of work I had created. This is why I was hired as a manager of a large publishing company. They were converting all of their cut and paste materials onto computers. Prior to that, they had outsourced this type of work, but new technology gave them an opportunity to bring all of that activity in-house. I was brought in to hire and train staff on how to create the images, perform color corrections, produce magazine page-layouts, etc."

Apple Computer had just released the Power Macintosh, a new line of personal computers that were cutting edge. They were expensive computers to afford and not too many people could learn how to apply the new technology.

"My first year, I received three salary increases. They were afraid that I would take one of the many offers that were being made by competing companies," recalls Maggie.

"Eventually publishing began to downsize. For instance, the company I worked for went from 500 to 350 to 200 to 150 people. There was a decrease in advertising income, but a lot of the downsizing was caused by faster and better computers."

Leaving the World of Publishing

Her decision to leave her position at the magazine was two-fold. When she was offered a high position, out of a pool of several hundred applicants, she realized that this would likely result in the elimination of her original boss's job. Out of respect for him, she gradually transferred her work to him and helped train him on the new work needing to be done.

"I knew that it would be much easier for me to find work in the marketplace than it would be for him," recalls Maggie.

A secondary motivation for Maggie was that she recognized that she had reached the top of her field, and that there was no room for an increase in salary. She took the advice of her husband, Chris Wang, and became a data base administrator (DBA).

Like a Good Neighbor

Maggie first met Chris in 1993 in Queens, New York, where they were neighbors. They had a lot in common. Both were born and raised in China, were studying computer science, and living in Queens.

Chris had graduated from college in China at the young age of 18 when he went to work for the government. He arrived in America in 1986, as an exchange student. Chris worked on a farm in Vermont with the original intention of returning to his homeland to apply what he had learned. Instead, he took a job as a bookkeeper with a jewelry company, and enrolled at Queens College to learn how to become an IT network engineer.

Maggie was paying $450 per month for her one bedroom apartment in Queens, and would take the subway to NYIT, located across the street from Central Park.

The two neighbors met, and were married a year later.

First Impressions

When Maggie first arrived in the United States, she was not very excited. Everything seemed very old and very crowded.

"I wanted to turn around and go back to China," says Maggie. "But Jeva got very upset. She said, 'I just spent $5,000 to bring you here, and you don't even give it a chance?' So, I gave it some more time."

"Jeva was very helpful to me," recalls Maggie. "I stayed with her when I first arrived and then was able to work as a cashier in Jamaica, a working-class neighborhood in Queens."

Venturing Into Real Estate ... Out of Necessity

Maggie transferred into the mortgage lending business, but stopped working in 2003 to stay home with her son and daughter, Aaron and Eileen. Five years later, however, it became apparent that changes were being made at Chris's company, and the threat of being laid off was real. "Inherent in the IT industry is that things change so quickly. Depending on the situation, your knowledge can become obsolete," says Maggie.

"We have never been people who obsess about money. There

is no huge desire for us to make more and more money. We are content with the simple life. But, we decided to invest in real estate because we wanted to be less dependent on Chris's job," says Maggie.

With the looming threat of a job layoff, Chris and Maggie sold much of their stock portfolio and purchased real estate. Maggie used the knowledge she had picked up in the mortgage lending business to put together a plan of buying tired properties and making renovations that increase their value.

"Many of the properties that come available have been owned by the same family for several generations. By the time they come on the market, they need a lot of work done on them. The biggest challenge is working effectively with the contractors to do the work quickly and affordably," says Maggie.

She discovered that while she doesn't like chasing dollars, she does like chasing her passion, which includes turning around real estate.

Maggie says, "Real estate is like a blank piece of paper. Just like adding watercolors and paint, you envision those things that can make your property beautiful."

The Rest of the Story

Eventually, Chris was laid off … and found another position the same week! Maggie smiles, "We thought that finding another job would be a more difficult thing to do. But, we are glad we got into real estate anyway. It added another investment vehicle. Today, we could sell the real estate and realize our profits, but why would we do that? It's working very well."

She adds, "Owning real estate doesn't change our life. It just gives us more options in a volatile job market."

One lesson Chris and Maggie have learned is that real estate is unpredictable. "At the time we made our purchases, the real estate values seemed very expensive to us. We didn't realize it at the time, but we were actually buying at relatively low prices."

Another lesson they learned was the importance of making life a little bit easier by avoiding long term debt. "We always made it a priority to pay down our house loans. When we decided to buy real estate, we had already paid off our home. This was a real advantage for us," Maggie recalls.

Today, Chris and Maggie live in New Jersey with their son, Aaron, who enjoys playing tennis, and Eileen, an accomplished fencer. In their free time, the family enjoys reading books, watching movies, travelling, and playing tennis.

Maggie has already located the first New York property for her sister, Jeva, and the *bountiful investors*, and she remains on the lookout for other exciting real estate properties.

This time, less out of necessity … more for pleasure.

Other Stories and Conversations

What All Great Real Estate Professionals Have in Common

On my blog at www.GarrettScanlon.com, I share stories from some of the most successful real estate pros in the Midwest. After observing their careers and listening to their stories, I tried to answer this question: *Other than their sheer success, what do all of these winners in the world of real estate have in common?*

While these qualities pertain to people who make real estate their *fulltime* profession, the *bountiful partners* in this book also possess these entrepreneurial characteristics. This is what I learned:

Each one of them is very good at creating structure in an otherwise *un*structured environment. Real estate is not your typical 9 to 5 job, where opportunities are clearly identified and day-to-day responsibilities are well defined. It is up to the *real estate professional* to identify the problems and opportunities. It is up to *them* to set a plan of action that will provide solutions and fill voids in the marketplace.

Step by step, they implement their plan over the course of weeks, months, and years. They are not told how they should allocate their time, or which deals they should pursue or ignore.

For better or worse, *they* make the decisions. Their time and efforts are always at risk, because typically, they are only rewarded if their choices and decisions result in success. The cost of success or failure is theirs. That is why a *Single Page Life Plan for Realtors* is such a valuable tool for real estate professionals.

All of them share the characteristics of creativity, optimism, confidence, and persistence. Not all were particularly good students in school, not all are consistently hard workers, and not all are exceptionally talented. But they all know how to teach themselves what they need to know to excel, can focus a lot of energy on important tasks at hand, and they all know how to work effectively with other people.

They demonstrate a willingness to make decisions and to incur risk. There is little, if any, guaranteed income.

Most importantly, without exception, all of the successful real estate people seem to succeed in very unique and different ways from each other. They all take *different* paths, *thereby taking advantage of their individual skills and talents.* There is not one formula for success to follow, but hundreds! This is why it is almost impossible to predict, out of a group of newcomers to the world of real estate, which individuals will ultimately succeed. The *commonality* among these high achievers is that they all take a *unique* approach to their business.

A Farming Attitude

Author's Note: *Below is an excerpt from my real estate blog at www.GarrettScanlon.com. I included this story because it ends with a comment that is in-line with the theme of this book. Don Ray is a real estate investor who has become a good friend of mine over the years. Meeting people like Don is what has made the real estate profession such a wonderful time for me. Here is Don's perspective.*

Don Ray is a real estate investor who takes a positive and hopeful attitude to what the future will bring. Don's education began on a farm in Tennessee. It was there that he and his five brothers farmed 180 acres with the bare essentials of farm equipment.

Don recalls, "We had no electricity, little running water, and few tools. We plowed the fields by mule. It was very difficult work, for sure. Looking back, my father probably thought that the hard, long days of labor would keep me and my brothers out of trouble. And he was probably right."

"But as 'country' as this might sound, I really formed a concept of investment on that farm," says Don. "We planted corn, watermelon and tomatoes. Basically, we tried a little bit of everything. And I discovered you *really* do reap what you sow. Some plantings die off completely, some have average results, and others do great! I learned that you cannot expect a 100% harvest of everything you sow. But more importantly, I learned that if you do not sow anything, you do not have any chance at all of a harvest. That is how I always viewed the businesses I started and the real estate properties I purchased."

Don says, "They will not all grow to your expectations, but some of them will do fine and others will pleasantly surprise you. But nothing will mature and ripen if you do not plant any seeds at all. The more seeds you plant along the way, the greater your opportunity is for a bountiful harvest."

The Get Rich Slow Method

Investing in real estate has been described by some as the *get rich slow method.* While there is often an immediate cash flow return on a person's investment, a strong return from real estate also depends on the property appreciating over time. When I think of power of appreciation, I am reminded of the buyer who had incorrect cash flow expectations from an investment property she was about to buy.

Years earlier, she and her husband had invested in land that had subsequently appreciated in value. After her husband passed away, she sold the land to a single-family homebuilder and decided to use the proceeds from that sale to buy income-producing apartments.

With a wonderful smile, she looked across the closing table and asked, "Now Garry, explain to me again how much cash flow I should expect from this investment."

We had discussed this earlier at length, and I replied, "Again, it is only an estimate, but your cash flow should range somewhere between $7,000 and $8,000."

"That's right," she said. "Now, should I expect that same amount *every* year?"

I was incredulous. Surely, we couldn't have come this far without having communicated a clearer understanding of her return-on-investment. "No," I responded. "That will be your cash flow every *month*!"

She raised her eyebrows and dropped her jaw. In disbelief, she turned to her real estate agent, seated at her right and asked, "Is that right?"

He confirmed that it was indeed her anticipated monthly cash flow. She looked around the table to see if there was some mistake. She then looked at me again and asked, "So, what you're telling me is that I could essentially retire?"

Throughout the rest of the closing, we were all just going through the motions. All of us had just experienced the pleasure of watching someone, right before our eyes, realize their investment dream. Years of real estate investment had suddenly culminated in a life-changing event.

The get rich slow method, of planting seeds and patiently waiting for a harvest, turned out to be very bountiful that day.

Walking and Talking

A Story for Someone Who is Beginning a Career in Real Estate

People sometimes ask me how I got my start in investment real estate.

In the late 80s, I joined a group of 25 brokers at Coldwell Banker Commercial Real Estate. One of those brokers was Wayne Harer. Wayne had played ten years of minor league baseball for the Red Sox and Yankee organizations and, one season, actually won the AAA Batting Crown with a .350 batting average. Unfortunately, that was not enough to replace American League MVPs Freddie Lynn and Jim Rice, or Hall of Famer Carl Yastrzemski from their spots on the roster.

I considered Wayne a 'veteran' commercial broker because he had all of two years of experience leasing downtown office space.

One day as he was walking through the lobby, I called out, "Hey Wayne, do you have a couple of minutes?"

"Walk with me, talk with me!" he said as he got on the elevator.

"What?"

"C'mon Scan. Walk with me, talk with me. Let's go!"

Being new in the business, I jumped at the invite. Not only was Wayne a successful broker, he was the only guy I knew who had his own baseball card!

I spent the next 2 hours tagging along with Wayne as he conducted business downtown. He visited a dozen offices, dropping off brochures, asking to talk with tenants and owners. A business card handed out here, a "Howyabeen" there. We took elevators and escalators; we cut across parking lots and through retail stores. I kept asking Wayne real estate questions. Wayne kept walking and talking.

Five miles later, it was obvious that Wayne knew every floor of every downtown building, every owner, and every tenant. He knew everyone by name; the secretaries, the lobby clerks, even the policeman on the corner. You were never a stranger for long when 'Wayno' was *walking and talking.*

Wayne said, "When I was hired by Coldwell Banker, they told me, 'You are going to be an office broker.' That sounded great to me, but I really didn't know what they meant. When I asked them exactly what an office broker did, they pointed outside their office window and said, 'Do you see all of those buildings out there? You are going to learn everything there is to know about every single floor of every single building.'"

"They told me I needed to meet with every tenant leasing agent, property manager, lender, and owner associate with those buildings; that I needed to find out all of the square footages, the rental incentives being offered, the type of tenant improvements being done and the details of every lease."

Wayne added, "That can seem like a daunting task for a new real estate agent, fresh out of professional baseball. It took me about 18 months to do that groundwork. And it is groundwork! Your energy level has to be very high. When you start at the top of the LeVeque Tower and start working, floor by floor, it can be exhausting."

One time someone asked Wayno, "What if there is a no-solicitation sign outside the office?"

"Better yet!" he replied. "That means there is a good chance all of the other brokers were scared off. The reality is, if you haven't been thrown out of every building in your territory at least once, then you're not doing your job."

The questions I had for Wayno that day were insignificant compared to the education he gave me, *walking and talking.* This is what it is all about; getting face-to-face and personal with the people with whom you want to do business.

He not only became familiar with the product, inside and out, but also grew to know the individuals who would later become his customers. Certainly, there were scores of agents "working the phones", making calls to potential clients, but there is no substitute for meeting face-to-face the way that Wayne Harer demonstrated.

As of early 2005, the major issue for tenants choosing office space became one of human resources. According to Wayne, "Business owner's main emphasis when choosing space is how it will affect their ability to hire talented professionals. Today, they value the building-design, parking, prestige and location of office space in terms of how they can use their office space to lure employees from competing businesses and/or from other areas of town. Before, their only consideration had to do with their customers. Now they want their office to attract the best personnel; the best sales agents, or attorneys, or financial planners, or architects, etc. to their company."

As his business has expanded Wayne schedules luncheons with members of development departments and chambers of commerce. He gives presentations to small groups of brokers, company executives and building-owners. He has built a "team" of space planners, tenant improvement contractors, legal and financial analysts, and marketing specialists to provide service to those clients with whom he still gets face-to-face.

Today, Wayne still sports a couple of AAA World Championship Rings from his day with the Columbus Clippers in the early 80s. He has been honored 12 out of the last 13 years as the Highest Volume Commercial Sales Leader in Columbus … walking and talking!

Live Prosperously, So Others May Prosperously Live

Below is an excerpt from www.GarrettScanlon.com

I remember the first time I saw a bumper sticker that read: "Live simply so that others may simply live." My first thought was to place another bumper sticker next to it that read: "And live prosperously so others may prosperously live."

One day, I was volunteer-teaching a class of 8th grade students about the benefits of living in a prosperous economy. I said, "I love the fact that doctors earn a lot of money. Any guesses as to why I do?"

One student answered that it was because our health is very important, and earning a good income is a good incentive for talented people to make the effort of attending medical school.

Another student took a poke at me. "I know *why* you like the fact that they make a lot of money. Because then you can sell them real estate!" We all laughed, and I agreed that it was true. I then asked if anyone else in the class could think of another reason why it was a good thing that doctors earned a good income.

An arm shot up and started waving left and right. "Oh! Oh! Oh!" He could hardly contain himself before I called on him.

"I like it, because my dad's a doctor!"

"That's a good reason too," I said.

An Economic Boom and Increased Charity

During the economic boom that took place under Ronald Reagan in the 1980s, people were left with control over more of their hard earned dollars. True to form, they responded with tremendous generosity to those less fortunate. Charitable giving more than doubled during those years.

Prior to Reagan's leadership, there was a lot of suffering caused by high inflation, high interest rates, and high unemployment. Many people who owned businesses and farms lost everything during the recession. It was a very bleak time during the economic recession of the late 70s.

For some reason, however, people will sometimes look back on such times and assign a sort of romanticism to a slow sputtering economy. They forget the suffering that it can bring.

But when things turned around in the 80s, there is one thing we discovered; Prosperity is contagious! By pointing to the success happening in America, Margaret Thatcher was able to get reforms passed in her country that also brought great prosperity to the British people. Prosperity also spread to other countries across the globe.

Jobs were available again, low interest rates made houses more affordable, and inflation was cut in half. The standard of living increased, the air was made cleaner, and interest rates were reduced from 21% to single digits.

The Impact on the *Bountiful Partners*

The impact it had on the *bountiful partners* was extraordinary. They arrived in America either in the midst of the economic boom of the 80s, or shortly thereafter. Job opportunities were plentiful, inflation had been corralled, and interest rates were in the single digits once again.

Many of them entered the world of technology and innovation that surged during those prosperous years. The new economy provided venture capital that fueled huge advances in that industry.

The Many Forms of Prosperity

All of us are able to create prosperity in our lives. Prosperity is not just limited to financial success. As many of the *bountiful partners* attest to in this book, true wealth comes in the many ways we can help others. As leaders of our families, the more successful you become financially, physically, and spiritually the more prosperity you will be able to share with others.

The Five Elements of a *Single Page Life Plan*

Real estate people tend to be entrepreneurs. If you are reading this book, in all probability, you have an entrepreneurial spirit. If so, it is important to add structure to the unstructured world of investment real estate.

That is why I created the *Single Page Life Plan* concept. It has helped me and others add intentionality to our day-to-day life. I hope it is beneficial to you.

Visit my website to learn more about *Single Page Life Planning*, and to access tools that will help you create your own plan.

The idea is to *discover the simple*, like Einstein did. He sculpted away the clutter and left us with the meaningful. He chipped away at row upon row of mathematical calculations and left us with $E=mc^2$. He simplified complexity! It wasn't easy, but better.

The idea is to discover, and focus on, the truly meaningful things in your life; the significant things that matter. The *Single Page Life Plan* is designed to help you do that in a fast, fun, and creative way.

There are 5 elements to the *Single Page Life Plan*

1. Mission or Vision Statement
This is the overarching vision you have for your life. All other parts of your plan synchronize with this.

2. Life Categories
Your life categories are the six major highways that lead a path towards your vision statement. These life categories are what you consider to be the most vital aspects of your life.

3. Action Steps
These are the specific, achievable, and measurable steps that you commit to take on a daily basis to remain intentional, strategic, and accountable to each of your life categories.
Action steps turn your life vision into reality.

4. The Boxes
There are four Boxes to your plan:

- *Coins* are small kindnesses you perform to help others you encounter along your path.
- *Attitudes* speak to the frame of mind you adopt to stay motivated in your quest.
- *Potholes* are hurdles and distractions that steer you away from your goals.
- *Strengths* are the character attributes, skills, and talents you possess that can propel you towards attaining your goals.

Finally, there is the fifth and final element of your life plan:

5. Your Signature
This is the part of your *Single Page Life Plan* that will take the least amount of time, but will have the longest term of consequence. It is the promise to yourself that you will follow the vision you have for your future.

The above is an excerpt from my book Single Page Life Plan. *Visit* **www.GarrettScanlon.com** *to download tools to help you create your own plan!*

A Conversation with Spring Property Management

Owning and operating real estate is owning a business. As such, the management of the day-to-day operations is essential. Below are the thoughts and comments of people who are in that arena week in and week out. This is a summary of a conversation I had with them.

Overall Philosophy or Mission Statement

In a sentence or two, please describe the overall mission statement for Spring Property Management.

Spring Property Management was founded on the principle that a resident's home is their castle. With this in mind, we are committed to providing our residents with the highest standards of client service.

Regarding Leasing

How do you attract tenants?

Our primary methods of advertisement are on paid websites such as ApartmentFinder, ForRent, and ApartmentGuide as well as Craigslist.

What is your screening process for tenants?

We require all prospects over the age of 18 to fill out a rental application, turn in one month's worth of pay-stubs, a copy of their photo ID, and a copy of their social security card. We then contact their current/previous landlord to verify if their rental history has been satisfactory or not. We will also contact their employer to verify their employment history if there are concerns in that regard. We also pull their credit history, credit score, and criminal background. This process helps to quickly weed out applicants who are unqualified and significantly decreases the number of evictions and other costly expenses.

What are typical tenant demands? What amenities are most important to residents in the price range you are in?

The two questions I hear most frequently are "Do you have a pool?" and "Do you have a workout facility?" The funny thing about those questions is that the vast majority of residents rarely if ever use those amenities. Swimming pools are an easy way to entice tenants with children and gyms are helpful in swaying young adults to rent with you.

It is becoming increasingly prevalent that tenants require a way to pay their rent electronically, whether that be through an online resident portal or point of service credit card processing.

The amenity demands are also dependent on the price range. Our lower priced communities tend to prefer low rents in exchange for few, if any, amenities. Our mid-grade properties typically have a swimming pool and a discounted membership to a local gym. Our luxury properties have a pool and workout facility on site, as well as monitored security alarm service and even free basic cable at some locations.

How many tenants are allowed in each apartment?

While at this time there are no Fair Housing laws regulating the number of people allowed per apartment, we typically allow a maximum of two people per bedroom.

How do you time your initial lease, in terms of lease expiration dates?

A twelve-month lease is standard in this industry, however that is not always practical in Ohio. We typically offer one-year leases from March through September. If we have vacant apartments in the winter, we will usually offer anywhere between 6 month and 18 month leases. Let's face it, no one wants to move when it's 10 degrees outside with a foot of snow!

How often do you evict tenants you place?

Eviction rates depend on the property. Our luxury properties usually have one or two evictions per year. Our mid-grade properties will see maybe 5 or 6 evictions in a given year. For our lower end properties, there may be as many as one or two a month.

How does your renewal system work?

We require 60 days written notice to vacate an apartment; as such we begin sending renewal offer letters to tenants approximately 90 to 120 days prior to the end of their lease. It seems early to many people, however we have found that sending out renewal offers earlier can often secure more return rentals than sending them out at the last minute.

Our renewal letters are sent out in the first week or two of each month and they expire on the last day of the month. The expiration surprises some folks, but this can be very helpful to management if they are offering renewal specials such as free rent or complimentary carpet cleanings. It is very common for residents to turn in renewal letters well after the expiration date, but they may be unaware that the renewal special has changed. Clearly noting the expiration date on the offer letter helps deter unnecessary extensions of renewal offers and also can help to create a sense of urgency for the resident to come in and renew their lease.

Our company typically discounts the rental rate when tenants move in, which means that when their lease is up for renewal, they are below the market rate for the apartment. As a result, we then raise their rental rate between $20 and $50 on average when they renew their lease.

What is your process for turning a unit?

Our collections and turnover specialist walks through each vacant apartment to take notes and pictures on any damage or items left behind. We recommend taking photos as this gives you evidence if a past tenant attempts to refute any charges taken from their security deposit. We also highly recommend having the employee who walks the vacant units also be the employee who drafts up your security deposit refund letters as they are more likely to accurately charge the residents. It is easy for charges to be missed if the walk-throughs and refund letters are not completed by the same person.

Once the unit has been walked, a maintenance technician goes in and completes a punch out. This includes throwing away any trash or belongings left behind, patching nail holes, replacing items such as mini blinds, outlet cover plates, stove drip pans, light bulbs, door stops, et cetera. They also verify that all appliances are in working order as well as the HVAC system.

Next the painting contractor is scheduled to paint the unit, followed by the cleaning services vendor, then the carpet cleaners or carpet installers. We have the maintenance technician then complete a final walk through to ensure that the vendors' work has been completed and the apartment is ready to rent.

How long does this typically take?

Ideally we prefer a unit be fully turned within three to five business days. Sometimes that is just not possible, but all units are usually done within 3 to 5 days of move out.

Maintenance

If you have a preventative maintenance program, what is it? Ex. Replacing furnace filters, unit inspections.

Each spring we inspect the HVAC systems and replace the furnace filters.

What is your process for handling repair requests? How do residents make requests? (Via Email, stopping by the clubhouse, calling, other?)

Residents can call, stop by the office, email a staff member, or submit a maintenance request through our online resident portal. Once a request is received, we mark it as high priority (needs completed within 1 business day), medium priority (needs completed within 3 business days), or low priority (needs completed within one week).

Who does the work?

Our maintenance technicians handle 99% of our work orders. In the summer we will occasionally use a contractor for some of the more intricate HVAC repairs.

What kind of work do you contract out to third-party vendors and contractors?

Typically we contract out painting, vacant unit cleans, carpet cleaning/installing, snow removal, landscaping, lawn mowing, lake/pond treatments, large electrical projects, and more intricate HVAC problems.

Management Software

What kind of property management software do you use?

We currently use Yardi.

What tools does it have that helps to keep you organized? Proactive? Other?

The issue list function is probably the single most useful organizational tool. It allows the user to organize the work orders by property, priority, age, et cetera. It also has a function to mark work orders as "work in progress" if it is an ongoing project. The tickets can also be linked to the resident or unit accounts, which is helpful in tracking persistent problems. The issue list function greatly diminishes the amount of missed or forgotten tickets and is also great at helping to plan out your maintenance technician's day to maximize their efficiency.

What reports do you generate for your own use?

On a daily basis, we generate the unit availability listing, the issue list, the balance due list, and the customer wait list. On a monthly basis we draw up a renewal spreadsheet, an issue-list reconciliation, and other various occupancy reports.

What reports do you generate for the property owners?

Typically an owners statement is sent out which includes bank statements, a profit & loss recap, a listing of charges for maintenance expenses, etc.

How does a property management company add value for an owner?

We believe that the most important value a property management company gives an owner is peace of mind. Many first time owners do not realize the extent of the work required in property management. The work does not end once you post and deposit the rent check on the first. That's only the beginning. Neighbor disputes, 2AM emergency maintenance calls, rent nonpayment issues, keeping a high occupancy rate during the slow winter season...these are all the "not so fun" parts of property management.

When an owner invests in a quality property management firm, they are really helping to give themselves a peace of mind regarding their investment.

A property management company also gives an owner access to years of knowledge and experience. If you combine the years of experience for each of our company's employees, we have a total of over 65 years. That is a lot of time and knowledge!

What is the most rewarding part of being part of a property management team?

Assisting customers in finding the right home for the next phase of their lives. We've had numerous residents over the years send us "thank you" gifts because we were able to help them get approved for a home they might not have been able to purchase without our help. Many times clients are looking for an apartment because of an upheaval in their life, such as a divorce or a job transfer. It is always a good feeling to know that you have helped alleviate some of their stress and fear, and made their transition as smooth as possible.

Final Thoughts

Many of the *bountiful partners* manage their own investment real estate, in addition to the real estate they own with the *bountiful* partnership. By doing so, they were required to learn the ins and outs of advertising, leasing, preparing documents, overseeing maintenance and repairs, and keeping accounting records, etc. The *benefit* is more control. They also improve their cash flow by avoiding property management fees, and other expenses. The *detriment* is that property management takes a lot of time and can be stressful.

Some owners ease into the process. For instance, if they own 10 properties, they might manage one or two themselves, until they get the hang of it.

Performing property management is a personal decision. Hopefully, this conversation with Spring Property Management will help you decide what is best for you if you ever decide to purchase investment property.

Preparing Others for a Successful Future

One of the things I have learned about the partners profiled in this book is how much they value giving back to their communities. Among other activities, many of them have become very committed to the success of the Ohio Chinese School.

The Ohio Chinese School was established in 2013 to provide an educational platform and cultural center for the growing Chinese community, and the diversified general public, in Columbus, Ohio. The school provides enrichment opportunities and a welcoming environment for students to learn the Chinese language and culture. They provide weekend classes that teach the essence of Chinese tradition, such as history, culture, social practices, arts and crafts, music and dances, Kung Fu, Taichi, etc.

The principal of the school, Ms. LiChun 'Spring' Zhang, was instrumental in the initial startup of the school. According to Jeva Lin, Spring is multitalented at structuring classroom studies, scheduling, advertising, promotion, overseeing special events, and other things required in operating a school. According to Jeva, "She really created and grew a tremendous team around her. She is very smart and personable. That is a great combination!"

The school is staffed by extraordinary teachers who assist students in after-school programs, SAT/ACT preparation, and individual tutoring in math and English.

Talent Courses and History Classes

The school helps students become familiar with Chinese culture and to appreciate the beauty of Chinese arts. They offer courses in art, calligraphy & painting, drawing & sketching, speech & debate, origami, guitar & guzheng, folk dancing, martial arts, tai chi, chess, go, etc.

Additional classes dive deep into China's interesting and exciting history. From ancient traditions to geographical changes, students learn about all the developments that brought China to where it stands today. They also explore ancient Chinese classics that teach children traditional Chinese rules of behavior and discipline for success.

Adult Courses

For adults who are interested in learning Chinese language and cultures, the school offers *Chinese as Second Language for Adults.* They also provide courses aimed at helping people improve their overall health, such as yoga, taiji, karaoke, ballroom dance, chess, and go.

Activities

The school celebrates the Lantern, Moon, and Dragon Boat Festivals. They have bridge tournaments, where the best bridge players in the Central Ohio Chinese community teach newcomers to learn the game. There are picnics in the summer, Thanksgiving dinners in the fall, and a Chinese New Year's celebration in the winter.

Last year, the Ohio Chinese School held its first teacher appreciation Christmas party on a snowy afternoon in December. It was a great way for the families of the management team, teachers, and distinguished representatives of the Chinese community to gather together for a wonderful celebration of the holidays. The backdrop of a lighted Christmas tree surrounded by numerous gifts behind the smiling parents and children was a lovely sight to see. As the younger ones surrounded the warm fireplace, a potluck meal was arranged and provided by the management team and the teachers of the school for everyone to enjoy. Events like these are a great way for the staff, teachers, and families to bond and create a feeling of community; to enjoy each other's company.

The Shamrock Club

I have always considered it a great honor for me and my wife, Sherri, to be invited to various special events at the school. It reminds me of my Great Uncle Tony Scanlon, whose grandparents hailed originally from Ballylongford, Ireland. As much as he loved America, it was important for him to remember the customs and history of "the old sod". So, he was one of the founding members of The Shamrock Club in Columbus, Ohio, that celebrates the Irish culture, and created The St. Patrick's Day Parade that continues to occur every March 17th.

I also admire how inclusive the school leaders are to the community at large, sharing with them the best parts of the rich history of the Chinese culture. Like my Uncle Tony, they embrace the activities of their local communities, while staying in touch with the traditions of their heritage.

And the Beat Goes On!

Jeva Lin, who along with other concerned parents and bountiful partners, was integral in getting the school off to a great start puts it this way. "It is really important for our children, and for generations down the road, that they know our story; that they know what came before them. They learn a lot about faith, family, discipline, and other traits that will make them more successful in their own lives."

For readers who would like additional information on the school, you can visit the website at www.OhioChineseSchool.org.

As Jeva says, "Keeping an eye on the past will help the students create a better vision for the future."

Bonus Material: Fundamentals of Multifamily Investment Real Estate

Three Ways Real Estate Generates a Return on Investment (ROI)

Hypothetical Investment Scenario:

Purchase Price:	$100,000
Down Payment:	$ 20,000
Loan Amount:	$ 80,000

ROI 1: Cash Flow

Cash flow consists of all collected income less any expenses related to the operating of the property, including annual debt service (loan payments to lender).

Example: 2-unit apartment building.

Income:		
2 Apts. x $550 (month) x 12 (months)	$13,200	
Less annual vacancy & unpaid rent	660	
= Collected rental income	$12,540	
Plus other income:		
Late fees	50	
Pet fees	50	
Cable TV & Water income	300	
Application fee & Credit report	40	
Washer/Dryer Income	200	
Miscellaneous	20	
= **Total Annual (Net Effective) Income:**	$13,200	**$13,200**

Less Expenses:		
Taxes	$1,800	
Insurance	500	
Lawn & Snow removal	200	
Trash removal	200	
Painting/Cleaning	300	
Maintenance/Parts & Labor	1,000	
Property Management Fee	660	
Legal and Accounting	210	
Reserve (future replacements)	530	
Additional Expense	400	
Total Expenses:	$5,800	**$5,800**
Equals Net Operating Income		**$7,400**
Less Annual Debt Service		**$5,756**
6% Interest Rate		
30-year amortization		
80% loan to value		
Loan amount ($80,000)		
= Cash Flow		**$1,644**
Cash-on-Cash Return:		
($1,644/$20,000 downpayment)		**8.22%**

ROI 2: Principle Reduction

Investors typically don't pay "all cash" for a property. Oftentimes they borrow money from a lender and sign a note detailing the terms of how the borrowed money is going to be repaid. The note is "secured" by a mortgage on the property, the property is considered to be encumbered, to be leveraged.

Amortization: Loans are typically paid back (amortized) over a period of several years. The shorter the amortization period, the faster the loan is paid back to the lender. Example: Loan Amount = $80,000 and 6% interest rate.

15-Year Loan

Disadvantages: Annual debt service is higher.

Cash flow therefore is less every year.

Advantages: Property is paid off earlier creating much greater cash flow after 15 years.

Equity in the property increases at a greater rate.

30-Year Loan

Disadvantages: Takes longer to pay off the loan.

Advantages Cash flow is higher in earlier years.

Decreased risk for negative cash flow throughout the period of ownership.

ROI 3: Appreciation

Appreciation is the increase in market value that occurs over the period of time the investors own the property.

Causes for Appreciation:

- Increases in monthly rental rates.
- Escalation in the cost of construction resulting from increases in materials and the cost of labor.
- Reduction in supply (this is often the result of a lack of remaining land available to build additional property).
- Increased government intervention, as municipalities grow, obtaining the proper zoning for new development becomes a lengthier and expensive process. Pushing up the cost of real estate.
- Lower interest rates allow a Buyer to justify paying a higher price for real estate.
- There is increased demand from investors fleeing alternative investments available to them.

The Role of Depreciation

Without the benefit of depreciation, an investor would be required to pay taxes on the entire amount of positive cash flow plus the amount of principal reduction that occurs each year.

However, the total real estate (less the amount of land) can be depreciated over a certain number of years. The amount of depreciation you are permitted to take each year offsets some of the otherwise taxable income, deferring the payment of some or all of the taxes due, into the future.

Eventually, when the property is sold, that amount of depreciation will have to be *recaptured* and taxes will eventually have to be paid. In the meantime, however, you have the use of those tax deferred dollars!

Consult your accountant to see if you are able to depreciate your real estate.

Creating Your Team

Investors need to create a team of experienced and trusted professionals to assist them with their acquisitions, financing, operation, and disposition of property.

- **Mentors & Advisors:** This consists of individuals with real estate experience who can help establish goals and objectives.
- **Real Estate Agents:** Help you search the market for available properties.
- **Attorney:** Prepares and reviews agreements, title issues, etc.
- **Accountant:** Prepares your returns and consult on tax issues.
- **Lender:** With a full menu of lending options to finance a variety of property types.

- **Investment Partners:** Help you take advantage of real estate opportunities that are too large for the investor to purchase individually.
- **Property Managers:** They manage the day-to-day operation of the property.
- **Title Company:** Search ownership history to insure that clear title exists. Helps coordinate closing activities such as escrow accounts, closing statements, the notarization of signatures, etc.
- **Insurance Agents:** Make sure that they are well versed in insuring investment real estate.
- **Property Inspections:** To inspect for construction defects, maintenance issues, pest infestation, etc.
- **Appraiser:** Help determine the market value of the property.

How to Locate and Select a Professional Property Management Company

- Get referrals from other business owners.
- Research the company's reputation by reading trade journals and by interviewing trade associations.
- Visit sites that are managed by the prospective company and talk with their leasing agents.
- Ask to see examples of the income and expense statements, various leases, and the contract they use.
- Research the advertising they place in newspapers or online.
- Require that they be licensed to manage real estate.
- Determine how accessible and responsive they will be to answer your questions and listen to your input.
- Determine if their price for management is competitive.
- Ask to see their written policy on complying with all fair-housing and civil rights laws.

Questions to Ask Your Lender

- What requirements must I satisfy to qualify for the loan?
- What documents must I provide you in terms of tax returns, net worth, statements, bank statements, credit card accounts, etc.?
- What is the cost for the application?
- What are my total costs to obtain the loan, including closing costs, studies, appraisal, origination fees, etc.?
- What other costs will I have before I obtain loan approval?
- How long will it take to receive loan approval and then to close the loan?
- What is the interest rate?
- Is the interest rate fixed for the duration of the loan or does it adjust?
- If it adjusts, when does it adjust and how is the future rate change determined?
- Is the loan assumable?
- Are their "caps" in place that limit how much the interest rate can change?
- Over how many years does the loan amortize? 10, 15, 20, 25, 30 years?
- Do you require that an escrow account be set up to pay taxes, insurance or reserves for replacements?
- Please explain the variety of loan "packages" I can choose from to finance my property acquisition.

Questions to Ask the Owner When Buying Apartments

I was in my office one day, when a real estate investor called me on the phone. He said, "Garry, one of my tenants moved out ... and they took the refrigerator with them! They said it was theirs."

Uh-oh.

I immediately called the seller, who explained that those particular tenants had previously sold their home, and so they had brought their own refrigerator with them. He had simply forgotten, and there was no mention of it in the lease.

"Garry, I just put the fridge that was in their apartment into storage, and used it the next time one of my other ones broke down." The seller replaced the refrigerator and everyone was happy.

If we had asked the seller, prior to closing, if he owned his appliances, it might have prompted his memory and helped us to avoid all of the hassle.

On the following pages are questions you can ask an owner prior to writing a contract. It is not an all-inclusive list but will get you started.

- How long have you owned the property?
- What is the breakdown of rental spaces?
  Efficiency Apartments
  One bedrooms
  Two bedrooms
  Three bedrooms
  Garages
- Are utilities available? Separately metered? Who pays?
- Who pays for the water bill reading-fee (if separately metered)?
- Who owns the trash dumpsters? Who pays for trash removal?
- Which appliances are available in each apartment?
  Range
  Refrigerator
  Dishwasher
  Microwave
  Washer/Dryer
  Smoke Detectors
  Other:______________________________
- Does the resident own any appliances?
- Is there air conditioning? Central / Sleeve / None
- What are the resident's criteria? Income qualification? Credit reports? Criminal reports? Is any current resident under eviction?
- Security deposits: Regular amount? Pet deposits? Non-refundable deposits?
- Leases: Length? Month to month? Late fees? Do you allow pets? Do you charge extra rent for pets? How many tenants have pets currently?

- Concessions: Have any future concessions been promised to the resident? Have any services been given to the residents? Are any other "freebies" given to the resident?
- Improvements made within the last two years: Roof? HVAC? Carpeting? Parking lot? Other?
- What is the current number of vacancies?
- How many residents have "given notice" that they'll be moving out?
- Service contracts: Are there any agreements that will survive a transfer of ownership?
- How long have the residents lived at the property?
- Have the apartments been condominiumized? If so, how much are the condo fees?
- Management: Who currently manages the property? How do they charge you? What percent of collected income do they charge you?
- Is the seller doing a 1031 like kind exchange into a replacement property?
- Who is the current lender? Is the loan assumable? Is seller-financing available?
- Do the residents rent any furniture or appliances from you?
- Do you lease anything that is used in the management of property?
- Do you maintain a model apartment?
- Is model furniture, pool equipment, desks, computers, etc. included in the sale?
- Are you the sole owner?

- Please supply me with the following information: Income/expense statements for the last two years. Current rent roll. Recent tax bill. Copies of all leases.
- Is there an existing survey for the property?
- Is there an existing environmental report for the property?
- Are there certificates of occupancy for the property?
- Are there any existing building plans for the property?
- Have historical maintenance records been kept for the property?

Just as important as asking questions to a seller, is learning about those things that you don't know that you don't know! That is why you **need to consult with an attorney** whenever you embark on the purchase of investment real estate.

The single most important thing you must take to every closing ... an attorney!

People ask me all the time, "Do I really need to have an attorney represent me?" The stand pat response for any Realtor to give is that yes, you should be represented by an attorney in the transaction. To be honest, 25 years ago, I didn't think that it was all that essential. But over the years, I have seen attorneys save their clients a lot of money, stress, time, *and disaster!* Maybe it is because there are more real estate laws, or maybe it is because the laws are becoming more complicated in nature; but my recommendation to anyone buying or selling apartments is, hire an attorney.

Having an attorney is simply the cost of doing business today!

Security Deposits

Owners (landlords) collect security deposits at the beginning of a lease, to be returned to the tenant (resident) only if rents have been paid in full and the apartment has been left in a condition consistent with normal wear and tear that is associated with someone living in an apartment.

Security deposits typically range from $100 to the amount of one month's rent. Security deposits that are not refunded to the tenant are used to pay towards damage made to the apartment and unpaid rent.

A Word on Pet Fees!

There are a lot of residents who are very attached to their pets. Below are some things to consider when working with them

- Limiting the rental of your property to those residents that don't have pets can result in fewer leases and less cash flow.
- Responsible pet owners can be excellent renters.
- Pet fees, unlike the regular security deposits are very often non-refundable.
- A modest increase in monthly rent, of between 5% and 10%, is typically charged to pet owners in anticipation of increased wear and tear. Pet fees are generally nonrefundable.
- Restrictions on the weight and/or breed of pets are common.
- Waste disposal companies are available, but typically this duty is reserved for the tenant.

When Interest Rates Change

There are dozens of changes that take place in the marketplace when interest rates change. The impact a change in interest rates will have on your real estate investment will depend on:

- Why they changed.
- What type of financing you have in place on the property.
- What terms and conditions you have on your loan.
- How long the change in rates continues.
- The part of the country you reside.
- Etc.

On the following page are just a few things to consider when rates go up or down. But they will vary along with the multiple variables in the marketplace.

When Rates Go Down:

- More people are able to afford the purchase of their first house.
- Existing renters move out to buy a house.
- Potential renters often choose to buy a house.

- Concessions and promotions increase to entice people to rent.
- Overall collected rental income is reduced as a result of this "softness" in the marketplace.
- Owners take advantage of the lower interest rates by refinancing their loan and reducing their monthly debt service.
- Reduced debt service helps to offset the loss of rental income.
- Market values of apartments typically remain strong because buyers are able to take advantage of the low interest rates at the time they make their purchase.

When Rates Go Up:

- Fewer people are able to qualify to buy a house
  - o House purchases are delayed
  - o Apartment leases are extended.
- Fewer apartments are constructed
  - o Financing becomes more difficult.
  - o Construction costs increase.
- Occupancy rates increase.
- Monthly rental income increases.
- Typically, a rise in interest rates is a response to inflation.
- Market values typically increase, especially for properties with assumable loans.
- Interest rates on adjustable rate loans adjust upwards.
- Annual debt service increases.

What is a Cap Rate?

You hear about Cap Rates (or Capitalization Rates) all the time, from people who buy and sell investment real estate.

When discussing cap rates, it might be in connection with the purchase price you *paid* for the property, the price you are *considering paying* for the property, or a price a seller is *asking* for the property (for instance sometimes you will hear, "They are asking an 8 cap for that property."). In each instance you are referring to the purchase price of the property *in relation to the NOI it generates.*

Simply put:

Cap Rate = Net Operating Income ÷ Purchase Price

Net Operating Income for an apartment property is basically:

All of the **income** that is collected from the property, such as:

- Rental Income
- Late fees
- Pet fees
- Application fees
- Water income

Less any **expenses** you would incur on the property, such as:

- Taxes
- Insurance
- Lawn & Snow
- Trash
- Replacement of appliances, HVAC, etc.
- Painting and Cleaning
- Etc.

What remains is your **Net Operating Income** (**NOI**).

The NOI ÷ Purchase Price equals your Cap Rate.

Cap Rate Examples for a Property with a $10,000 NOI:

- If a property is generating $10,000 per year, and you wish to sell that property for $100,000. You are seeking a 10 cap. That's easy enough to calculate in your head, right? $10,000 (NOI)/$100,000 (Purchase Price) = .10 (called a 10 Cap).
- If, however, you are only able to sell the property for $90,000, then it could be said that you sold your property at an 11.1 cap rate. This time the same $10,000 NOI is divided by the lower price of $90,000. $10,000(NOI)/$90,000 (Purchase Price) = .111 (called an 11.1 Cap Rate).
- Now, let's imagine that a bidding war breaks out on your property and you sell the real estate above your asking price. Let's say $111,000. If this happened then the appraiser would rightly say that the property t ransferred at a 9 cap. $10,000 (NOI)/$111,000 (Purchase Price) = .09 (called a 9 Cap).

The Higher the Price, the Lower the Cap Rate

As you can see from these examples, the higher the price, the lower the cap rate. The NOI is a fixed number at $10,000, because that is simply the NOI that is being generated from the property every year. Only the purchase price changes.

Therefore, if a buyer agrees to buy at the lower cap rate of 9, it simply means that they are willing to pay a higher dollar amount to receive the $10,000 NOI that is coming in each year. Conversely, if the buyer demands an 11.1 cap rate, based upon the property's annual NOI of $10,000, then they will pay less for it; in this example $21,000 less.

Why So Many People Are Confused about Cap Rates:

This is what throws a lot of people off—they forget that Annual Debt Service is not an expense. Because it is not an expense, annual debt service (ADS) has nothing to do with calculating a cap rate!

- Cap Rates don't care if you borrow money against the property or not.
- Cap rates don't care if you have an interest rate of 6% or 8% or 10%.

Cap rates only care about the relationship between NOI and purchase price.

Some accountants might say that I am looking at this wrong, but this is how I view this topic. If you take $100,000 down the street to your local bank and they pay you an interest rate of 1% - To me, you just invested your money at a 1 cap. If you take that same $100,000 and buy a couple of apartments that are netting you $5,000 each year in cash flow, then you have invested your money at a 5 cap.

The best way to always remember what is a cap rate

I always tell clients that the best way to remember what a cap rate is, is to assume that you are paying all-cash for the property!

Now of course, you will rarely pay all-cash, but to determine the cap rate, ask yourself, "If I pay all-cash for this property, what would be my annual return?" If you buy a property, all-cash, for $100,000 and the NOI is $7,500; you just bought that property at a 7.5 cap rate!

Conversely, if a property is generating $12,000 each year, and you are willing to pay a price that gives you a 6 cap, then you'll pay $200,000 for that property ($12,000 NOI/$200,000 (Purchase Price) = 6 Cap.

As you can see in the last example, the cash on cash return percent will also be 6. That's because, when you pay all cash for real estate, your cap rate is the same as your cash on cash return. Simply put, the cap rate is what your rate of return from cash flow would be if you didn't borrow any money to purchase it.

Five Major Factors that Impact Cap Rates

1. Interest rates.

The lower the interest rate a person can use to leverage his or her purchase, the lower the cap rate that person will typically pay for the property. That is because they are looking for positive leverage. For instance, for a great investment property, many investors like to borrow their funds at a lower rate than the cap rate they are buying at. If they buy a property at an 8 Cap, they want to finance the property at a 6-6.5% interest rate.

This results in a positive cash on cash return. The larger that spread becomes between the cap rate price they are paying, and the interest rate of the funds they are using to make their purchase, the more positive cash flow they make.

If interest rates increase to a number higher than the cap rates being paid in the marketplace, then negative cash flow is created, and few people want to buy real estate at a negative cash flow.

2. Quality of the property.

Buyers are willing to pay lower cap rates for a property if they believe that it will appreciate in value, continue to stay rented, garner increases in rental rates, physically stand up over a long period of time, and be relatively easy to manage.

3. Supply and Demand.

Not all investors purchase strictly for economic reasons. For the owner-occupied retailer, doctor, or office tenant, who believes they must be in a certain area for their business to prosper, the value of the building might become secondary – at which point limited supply in a particular area might drive down cap rates.

4. Like Kind Exchange Activity.

When there is a great deal of selling activity in a particular market, the desire to defer capital gains taxes, often result in a flurry of buying activity that drives down the cap rate.

5. Alternative Investments.

When competing investment rates from banks, the stock market, or pension funds, goes down, investors more easily rationalize accepting a lower cap rate when buying investment real estate.

Remember, Not All Cap Rates are Created Equal!

Be careful when negotiating a deal where everyone is throwing around the term 'cap rate'. When someone says to me for instance, "All I am asking for, for my property is an 8 cap? That's fair, don't you think?" My first thought is to learn how he or she arrived at NOI.

- Have they inflated income to reflect *street rents*, or are they using *actual rents* that they collected over the last 12 months?
- Did they include property management fees in their expenses? A very popular comment you will hear is, "We just manage it ourselves, and therefore we didn't put in a management fee."

But, if I *do* decide to hire a management company to run these apartments for me, I *will* have that expense! Also, if I am buying the apartments in partnership with other people, I will certainly want to be compensated for my managerial efforts.

Arriving at the All-Important Figure: NOI

The point is, there are dozens of ways to arrive at an NOI figure. Their way of calculating NOI is oftentimes different than yours or mine. And, even if they do calculate it the same way as we do, there are expenses we will have as new owners that the current owners do not have.

For instance, after the sale our tax rate will be based upon the new transfer price, which might be quite a bit higher than the assessed value currently being used to determine the property taxes.

The Cap Rate, and other ratios used to determine market value of investment property, can be found in my 6-page laminated flyer titled, Understanding the Fundamentals of Multifamily Property which will is available at my site:

www.GarrettScanlon.com

Real Estate Terms and Definitions

There are a lot of important terms and definitions in real estate. Here are just a few, to give you some examples.

If you are like most people, you will oftentimes hear unfamiliar words used by an attorney, or lender, or accountant; terms or phrases that you simply do not understand. Always ask others to clarify and define the words they are using, so that everything is clear for you. Too often, people will hesitate to do that, because they don't want to look ill-informed. That can make for mistakes that can be very costly to you. So, be quick to speak up so that everything is clearly communicated to you.

1031 Like Kind Exchange: The exchange of one property for another of like-kind, of equal or greater value.

Assessed Value: The value of the property as determined by local government to assess taxes

Balloon Payment Date: Date upon which the entire balance of a loan, or a substantial amount of the loan balance is due and payable.

Broker: An agent licensed to enter into an agency relationship to sell, lease, or manage property for a principal, without taking title to the property.

Capital Gains and Losses: The profit or loss from the sale of a capital asset.

Capitalization Rate: The rate of return generated by the net operating income as a percent of the purchase price (NOI/ Purchase Price).

Investor's Net Worth: The total assets of an investor less their total liabilities.

Lien: A charge made against property to securitize loans, taxes, mechanics, parts, and labor, etc.

Recording: Giving public notice of legal documents such as deeds, notes, mortgages, liens, etc. by recording them with government offices.

Seller's Affidavit: A sworn statement in writing, signed by the Seller, stating a certain set of facts.

Survey: A report detailing the quantity and boundaries of a piece of land.

Title: The union of all elements, which constitute proof of ownership.

Title Insurance: Insurance that protects against flaws in the ownership rights of a property.

Warranty Deed: Conveyance of title warranting certain assurances and guarantees.

Zoning: Government regulations specifying acceptable uses of land within a community.

Afterword

Spending time with the *bountiful partners* who contributed to this book, reminded me of what President Ronald Reagan said in his first Inaugural Address:

> "We have every right to dream heroic dreams. Those who say that we're in a time when there are not heroes, they just don't know where to look. You can see heroes every day going in and out of factory gates. Others, a handful in number, produce enough food to feed all of us and then the world beyond. You meet heroes across a counter, and they're on both sides of that counter. There are entrepreneurs with faith in themselves and faith in an idea who create new jobs, new wealth and opportunity. They're individuals and families whose taxes support the government and whose voluntary gifts support church, charity, culture, art, and education. Their patriotism is quiet, but deep. Their values sustain our national life."

A Road to Bountiful chronicles the steps of adventurous individuals who travelled along various paths that connect China and America. Through hard work, unyielding persistence, and a commitment to education, these *heroes in the marketplace* have achieved success that has created a better life for themselves, their families, churches, schools, and communities.

They did it in a way that is very Chinese.

They did it in a way that is very American.

May their journey continue along *A Road to Bountiful.*

About the Author

Garrett K. Scanlon is an investment real estate expert who has represented clients in the sale and purchase of over $388 million of multifamily, office, and retail property. He has also served as Director of Sales and Leasing for CASTO, one of the largest family-owned developers of retail shopping centers in America.

Garrett is an author who shares real-life stories from his experiences working with truly exceptional leaders in the marketplace. His books include *Walking and Talking—Stories of Success and Humor in the Real Estate World of Business, Single Page Life Plan,* and *Single Page Life Plan for Realtors.* Garrett also wrote a book on leadership, *Lead Like Reagan: Principles of Dynamic Leadership*, and a book for high school students titled *Seeing Past Friday Night.*

He is a past member of the Upper Arlington Library Board, and has served multiple years as a Junior Achievement In-Class Volunteer.

Garrett continues to counsel and represent buyers and sellers of investment real estate. He and his wife, Sherri, live in Columbus, Ohio, where they enjoy tennis, bicycling, music, traveling, reading, and writing.

To learn more please visit **www.GarrettScanlon.com**.